Rodford Barrat was born in 1946 and has led a varied life including work in both television and the theatre. He currently works as a numerologist who lectures on how to improve life by the use of numbers. He has contributed articles to various magazines and researched the ancient link between colour and the name, and the metaphysical effect of sound.

The *Elements of* is a series designed to present high quality introductions to a broad range of essential subjects.

The books are commissioned specifically from experts in their fields. They provide readable and often unique views of the various topics covered, and are therefore of interest both to those who have some knowledge of the subject, as well as to those who are approaching it for the first time.

Many of these concise yet comprehensive books have practical suggestions and exercises which allow personal experience as well as theoretical understanding, and offer a valuable source of information on many important themes.

In the same series

THE ELEMENTS OF

NUMEROLOGY

Rodford Barrat

ELEMENT

Shaftesbury, Dorset • Rockport, Massachusetts
Brisbane, Queensland

First published in Great Britain in 1994 by
Element Books Ltd
Shaftesbury, Dorset

Published in the USA in 1994 by
Element, Inc.
42 Broadway, Rockport, MA 01966

Published in Australia in 1994 by
Element Books Ltd
for Jacaranda Wiley Ltd
33 Park Road, Milton, Brisbane, 4064

Cover design by Max Fairbrother
Design by Roger Lightfoot
Typeset by The Electronic Book Factory Ltd, Fife
Printed and bound in Great Britain by Biddles Ltd,
Guildford & King's Lynn

British Library Cataloguing in Publication
data available

Library of Congress Cataloging in Publication
data available

ISBN 1–85230–574–6

CONTENTS

ACKNOWLEDGEMENTS

Thanks to: Lilian Barratt; Dorothy Price; Keith Mayle; Corinne Squire; Rodney James; Alan Bird; Edward Ephraim; Margie Kelly; Peggy Squire; Michelle Finn; my editor Julia McCutchen; and my agent, Doreen Montgomery, for her unerring guidance; and the many numerological authors without whose wisdom and insight I would have been unable to write this book. I am indebted to you all.

For my father,
Bert,
who is not forgotten

1 · INTRODUCTION

The whole heaven is a musical scale and number.

Aristotle

Numbers can speak. Their language is numerology: an ancient science that is a numerical analysis of life – your life. It is a practical system that can be used today; it helps the unfolding of spiritual insight and the attainment of material success. This sounds like the stuff of fortune tellers' dreams but the reason a belief in the power of numbers has existed for thousands of years is because it works. It is possible to prove this for yourself.

Numerology shows your motivation; it reveals your talents; it displays how you appear to other people. It maps the trends of each day: what is happening, what has happened, and why. It indicates what is to come. Using this language of numbers improves the quality of life spiritually, emotionally, mentally or materially.

This guide through its elements enables you to compile your own numerological chart or those of others. It is one of the simplest metaphysical systems to learn. Its simplicity is its power.

'Have you the grass that sings or the bird that is blue?' asks a character in *The Blue Bird*, a play by the Belgian writer, Maurice Maeterlinck. A search is made for this bird. Finally, it is found in its cage at home. It had been there all the time. The blue bird symbolizes happiness. Numerology shows, using numbers as symbols, how you can find your blue bird. You already have it. The numbers hidden inside your birthdate and name reveal your opportunities, abilities and talents. Knowledge of these symbols can create a happier life.

If you are familiar with natal chart astrology or other systems such as Japanese Ki or Chinese astrology, you will find numerology supports their findings. Each metaphysical science illuminates a part of your life in its own way. They are all mutually supportive. Numerology, similar to astrology in its analysis of your character, makes you think about yourself. This can sometimes be its most beneficial use.

Life can feel like being at an airport – sometimes we do not know which plane to catch – but by consulting our numbers we can know where we are headed. Numerology ensures we are prepared.

In this ancient science, cities, countries and towns have numbers assigned to their names. America vibrates to the number 5 and anyone with a 5 prominent in his or her chart would find living in America would further their aims. Great Britain vibrates to a 7 and Australia to a 3. These are generalizations. Yet, surprisingly, the *vibrations* of the numbers support the national stereotypes. Five seeks freedom, 7 is reserved, and 3 is a friendly, sociable number.

The word, *vibration*, is important. The theory of numerology rests on it. Everything in the universe vibrates and by using numbers – in the form of metaphysical arithmetic – we apply these vibrations as numbers to people, their names, their lives. Each number is a symbol that represents certain qualities. This is what this ancient belief or science is based upon. It has now been practised in differing forms for thousands of years.

The main system in use today is called Modern Numerology, or Pythagorean Numerology, and is based supposedly on the teachings of the Greek mathematician and philosopher, Pythagoras, who lived in the sixth century BC. This is the system described in this book. Although there are other numerological systems, all worthy of attention, this is the most popular and widely used. Each age selects the system that works best for its own time. This is ours.

The belief that numbers can symbolize concepts or reveal powers has been prevalent in many past civilizations. The Bible is full of number symbolism: 666 being the most famous. Scholars for centuries argued over its meaning: Martin Luther believed it foretold the length of the reign of the Popes; this was after the writer, Petrus Bungus, credited it as belonging to Martin Luther! It is now believed (by some) to represent the earthly mind of man.

The Chinese, the Egyptians, the Chaldeans, Greeks and Romans have all used their own numerological systems. The Chinese I Ching, which is thought to be over 4000 years old, states that odd numbers are light and even numbers dark. The Kabala, a system of ancient Jewish mysticism, reveals spiritual truths through its use of number, letter and sound. The Tarot also has numerological symbolism attached to it; and there is an old system of divination that uses numbers called Arithmancy. Recently, in 1955, the Runes had a form of numerology applied to them by Roland Dionys Jossé.

NUMEROLOGY TODAY

Numerology today is based on the ideas that disciples and followers of Pythagoras have handed down through the ages. The 'birth' of our present-day system and the beginning of its popularity is credited to an American woman, Mrs L. Dow Balliet. In the early years of the twentieth century she wrote two books equating the traditional symbolism of numbers with the English alphabet – a system for today. It was later refined and popularized by other numerologists, a Dr Julia Seton being among the most prominent. Numerology is again steadily gaining attention.

In *The Secrets of Numbers*, Lionel Stebbing writes: 'Numbers are not the cause of events but they illustrate the order and measure that is inherent in life'.

Previously, odd numbers were regarded as active or masculine, even numbers as passive or feminine; this can be related to the light and dark numbers of the I Ching. Today, we often find the correspondences of light/active given to *masculine* associations and dark/passive given to *feminine* as objectionable. Generally, the odd numbers are solo performers and the even numbers work at their best with others. The number 8 is a possible exception to this generalization. The nine numbers represent the following qualities:

1. Leadership. Initiative. Originality. Determination.
2. Cooperation. Diplomacy. Friendship. Kindness.
3. Self-expression. Creativity. Joy. Laughter.
4. Practicality. Self-discipline. Stability. Work.
5. Freedom. Communication. Versatility. Sensuality.
6. Harmony. Creativity. Responsibility. Domesticity.
7. Individuality. Intuition. Perfection. Contemplation.
8. Power. Independence. Ambition. Organization.
9. Compassion. Idealism. Great drama. Romanticism.

The zero or cipher is not considered in conventional numerology, although when lying behind a number it magnifies the qualities that number represents. In Indian numerology it is often considered unfortunate.

Some numerologists consider the numbers 11 and 22 should be considered separately from the nine digits above. This is dealt with briefly in Chapter 13.

It is enjoyable to classify people according to their Life Path Number – this is found in their birthdate (see Chapter 2) – and although all the numbers should be considered together, to illustrate the main qualities of the above numbers we will use nine examples: nine people whose public personas seem to match their single most important number, their Life Path:

Life Path 1 Mikhail Gorbachev
Life Path 2 Bill Clinton
Life Path 3 Bill Cosby
Life Path 4 Margaret Thatcher
Life Path 5 Mick Jagger
Life Path 6 Federico Fellini
Life Path 7 Diana, Princess of Wales
Life Path 8 Elizabeth Taylor
Life Path 9 Mahatma Gandhi

This, while interesting, should not be taken too seriously. Considering one number by itself is the same as judging someone by their sun sign in astrology, when the position of *all* their planets has to be considered.

Numbers represent certain qualities. We can see this when we look at the dates in the Gregorian calendar (the calendar now used by almost every country).

For the past one thousand years, the number 1 has held the dominant position. Each year has begun with 1. The 1 is associated with the masculine principle: the desire to lead, the desire to dominate. In our own civilization it has traditionally been man who has led and man who has taken the position at the top.

We now enter a new age: the number 2 takes up the position held by 1. The 2 has stood for cooperation, sensitivity and friendship and has been associated with women (because of this it has sometimes been considered a negative number – by men). It is no coincidence, when we consider the numbers numerologically, that the rise in the power of women – the feminist movement, the *weaker* sex being given the vote – has occurred as the number 2 is about to take over (2000 AD); an awareness of hidden forces, a realization of the rights of other species, the conservation of the land, all these movements are reflected in the change of the date. Numerology shows *it is* a New Age beginning. The Age of the 2.

The past century, 19--, has shown the power that is generated by the 1 and 9 together. The 9 reflects the humanitarian values that have grown during the last one hundred years; but 9 in its negative aspect symbolizes war and aggression. The 19 is known as a *karmic* number by some numerologists, signifying a battle for independence and a breaking away from past conditions. Naturally, the numbers of each decade will reflect the perceived theme.

The Nineties represent endings, change, great drama and humanitarian values uppermost: all shown by the number 9. The Berlin Wall fell in 1989; the date of the year had two 9s, the 1 and the 8 added together also came to 9. Three 9s, while representing the potential for change and idealistic action, can

5

create a severe disruptive influence. The last decade reflects this in greater criminal activity in many countries and social and civil disobedience on the streets.

The Eighties was a time of increasing material wealth in the West – the era of the 'yuppy'. Eight is a powerful number often associated with business and executive talents. It can make money (by working hard) but can become greedy. It gets what it deserves. You can write down the number 8 over and over again, without taking your pen off the paper. From wherever you start, you return back to the same place. Whatever the 8 does, it gets back. Many people who became rich (and greedy) in the Eighties, started to struggle in the Nineties.

In the Seventies, people liked to 'do their own thing'. It was the permissive age, a time for individualists. The number 7 needs to experience life for itself. It has to make its own mistakes. It usually does.

The Sixties heralded 'flower power', 'make love, not war'; the 6 brings harmony, balance, and loves beauty and colour around it. This number reflected the ideals of the 'flower children' of the period. The influence of the 9 in front of the 6 – 196- – brought many changes in the home, marriage and the upbringing of children.

In the Fifties, new and progressive changes and a need to feel free again took place. A pushing against boundaries. A curiosity about the world after the restriction of the 4 of the Forties.

The driving force behind each decade is seen when we analyse the numbers in the date. Important historical days can be examined to see if they reflect the character of the event.

The American Declaration of Independence, 7.4.1776, has three 7s (individuality, a dislike of being told what to do, a need to make its own mistakes) in the date, which also adds up numerologically (as you will discover) to the number 5. Five represents freedom, change, versatility. The name America also vibrates to this freedom seeking number, and the word 'independence' has seven of its twelve letters under the vibration of 5.

Rudolf Steiner, the Austrian philosopher, said: 'Those who

deepen themselves in what is called in the Pythagorean sense "the study of numbers" will learn through this symbolism of numbers to understand life and the world.'

The following chapters lead you through the principles of numerology. It is easy to understand and requires only simple addition and subtraction. Everyone has the skill needed to make accurate calculations.

Numerology books are often startlingly different in their approach to the subject. Glanced at casually, each book appears to contradict the next. This book details the main rules, the generally accepted principles of the subject. Authors with distinctive viewpoints can then be read with more informed interest.

Reincarnation and the purpose of *karma* influences some numerologists. You may believe or disbelieve in reincarnation but it is not addressed here. If *karma* applied to numerology particularly interests you, *Numerology for the New Age* by Lynn Buess is recommended as an informative and inspired read.

Predicting the future by numerology can never be 100 per cent accurate. The numbers reveal trends. When looking at a numerology chart you will make your *forecast* on what is *likely* to happen with the numbers you have. It is no more special or mystical than predicting the weather or deciding on stock market trends, although often more accurate. But it is a *forecast* nevertheless. It will be your *informed* opinion. There is nothing psychic about it. As you become used to using numbers, certain numerical spreads will reveal truths to you that less informed eyes would overlook. Numbers can be startlingly accurate when you know what they symbolize and can analyse their *probable* effects.

PERSONAL YEAR AND YOUR NAME

There are two controversial areas in numerology that deserve a mention. The first is the start of the Personal Year. The Personal Year shows the trends for each person for a period of twelve months. Some numerologists believe it starts on the 1st of January of each year, others on the date of a person's 'birthday'. I believe it is the former. You will be able, looking at past events in your own life, to form your own opinion.

Some numerologists believe the full name on the birth certificate (if you, have one) is the only accurate guide to the influence of your name. Thus if 'Baby Girl' is written on your birth certificate, in place of the name that you were eventually known by, then Baby Girl is the name that you will analyse. Others believe if your name has influence it has to be the name that you are known by: the name you use. I am certain this latter view is correct.

These contrasting opinions are mentioned here as some, but not all, books (a notable exception in this respect is the excellent *Numerology: Key to the Tarot* by Sandor Konraad) make absolute rulings about the start of the Personal Year and which name should be analysed without informing the reader about the divergent views on these two topics. You will as you read make up your own mind.

The easy way to learn the elements of numerology is to analyse yourself and it is recommended you note the attributes of your own personal numbers as you go along. A pattern will emerge. It can take you by surprise.

We first examine the numbers in your birthdate. These are important. They cannot be changed. The effect of your name comes next and influences what you want and how you carry out your plans. Finally we look at predictive numerology to see the trends in your life. There really is a right time, right place and right name. You will be able to find it.

FOUR RULES TO REMEMBER

1. Numbers have good and bad sides. They are symbols for positive and negative characteristics.
2. Each number is different – not better, nor worse, than others (this is the popular view, although some numerologists regard 4 and 8 as unlucky – perhaps because they work hard for their rewards!).
3. People with the same numbers have similar potential to work with. That is all. They do not react in exactly the same way.

4. Always consider all the numbers together: their combined effect. You are *never* represented by one number, even if it appears many times in your chart.

A healthy approach to number analysis is to remember there are aspects of life that numbers will not show. Are you good looking or ugly? Were you born rich or poor? Were traditional beliefs instilled in you from an early age? Do you live in a cold or hot climate? All these, and more, influence our behaviour. They must be considered alongside your numerological profile.

The English writer W. Somerset Maugham wrote: 'I recognize that I am made up of several persons and that the person that at the moment has the upper hand will inevitably give place to another. But which is the real one? All of them or none?'

Numbers can give you the answer.

2 · THE LIFE PATH

Consciousness of our powers increases them.

Vauvenargues

Your Life Path Number is your single most important number. It is found in your birthdate. In numerology it is as important as your sun sign is in Western astrology. While you should consider all your numbers, your Life Path represents the key to your whole chart. It is considered your 'lucky' number. Whether you can use its power easily depends on your supporting numbers. Following the direction of the Life Path makes life easier; ignoring it makes it hard. It shows your direction in life; the main opportunities you will attract; your talents and characteristics.

You will usually recognize the direction of this path. At times you may resist following it and refuse its opportunities. This is often the case if your Birthday Number (described in Chapter 4) is a different number. When this occurs, you can face 'problems' until you get your life back on track. Your friends may even recognize your birthday characteristics as 'more you', but this impression is untrue.

The meaning of the Sanskrit word *Dharma* could describe the function of the Life Path: the path to follow that accords with your essential nature. Each Life Path Number represents characteristics that are more likely to be displayed with that Life Path. We all have the ability to be leaders at different times in our lives, but it is Life Path 1 that will show this ability on a daily basis. It is these dominant traits and talents, appearing regularly, that distinguishes one Life Path from another.

To find your Life Path Number add all the numbers in your birthdate together. Continue to add the total together until only one digit is left. As an example, we will use the birthdate of the American civil rights leader, Dr Martin Luther King. Note that in America it is the month that comes first in the date, while in Britain it is the day.

Birthdate: 1.15.1929

$1+1+5+1+9+2+9 = 28 \quad 2+8 = 10 \quad 1+0 = 1$

Dr Martin Luther King's Life Path Number is 1.

This is the usual way to find the essence of numbers in numerology – continuing to add all the numbers together until only one number or digit is left. It is called *fadic addition*.

The Life Path is: the direction in life; the main opportunities that occur; the important talents and abilities. Or: what you can do; what you should do; and what will come to you.

LIFE PATH 1: THE LEADER

Direction: to learn to become self-reliant.
Opportunities: to lead or initiate projects.
Keywords: Leader. Initiator. Self-starter. Originator. Popular. Selfish. Egotistical. Dominating. Tyrant.

Ones have drive, determination and dash. They prefer to act rather than think. They need to improve their lives and with their good concentration can single-mindedly go after what they want. They want to do something rather than wait. They dislike sitting on the sidelines. Patience is sometimes a problem. They are often ambitious with leadership ability. They can make instant decisions but dislike seeing them changed by someone else. They possess strong beliefs combined with a forthright manner. There can be a dislike of team-work; they work best alone, although they are usually popular among their colleagues. In business they are self-assured with the

11

ability to handle their own problems. Original, brave and courageous, they dislike meeting opposition and will avoid it if they can.

Negatively: they are never satisfied with what they achieve and can be impatient. They are puzzled by people who are naturally slow starters. They can be uncomfortable with psychoanalysis and have difficulty accepting criticism. They hate arguments and to avoid them sometimes delay taking assertive action. This causes extreme frustration. In love, their determination to lead can desert them.

Life Path 1s that have shown the positive characteristics of leadership and courage are: Mikhail Gorbachev and Lech Walesa.

LIFE PATH 2: THE COOPERATOR

Direction: to learn how to cooperate.
Opportunities: to work well in partnerships or in groups.
Keywords: Cooperator. Friend. Diplomat. Inspired. Musical. Indecisive. Shy. Timid. Self-pitying.

Twos consider the feelings of others – sometimes before their own; they can let others take the credit that is their due. Although not natural leaders like 1s, they *can* lead but they like a strong partner beside them. They attract attention or celebrity in life. People are fascinated by the inspiration they communicate. They are masters or mistresses of timing and patiently wait until the time is right before proceeding. They dislike being hurried and should resist being forced to work at a pace that is uncomfortable. A love of music or musical ability is often present as they possess an accurate sense of rhythm. They are excellent at work that requires attention to detail. Always polite and courteous, they dislike coarse or rude behaviour. Diplomacy is a natural skill for 2s as they are able to see both points of view. They prefer to have a partner to share their lives with and can enjoy working in a team. Natural collectors and hoarders, they usually enjoy hunting around markets. They are honest people, with little need to flex their egos.

Negatively: there is difficulty in making decisions as they dislike upsetting anyone because they always see both points of view. If their emotions are stifled they eventually over-react. Sensitive and easily hurt, they can daydream too much. They can prefer to live out their fantasies in their minds rather than take action. Shyness or timidity can be a problem and they are uncomfortable if situations become too competitive.

Presidents Ronald Reagan and Bill Clinton are Life Path 2s, both appearing to have strong supportive partners. Showing 2's innate musicality are singers Diana Ross and Shirley Bassey.

LIFE PATH 3: THE ENTERTAINER

Direction: to learn how to create happiness.
Opportunities: to use creativity and imagination.
Keywords: Self-expressive. Gregarious. Creative. Lucky. Love-of-life. Vain. Restless. Easily bored. Jealous.

Threes are happy, enthusiastic bringers of joy. They light up the room. Imaginative, colourful people with creative ability, they have a natural wit and learn skills easily and quickly. There is a definite need for love in their lives. Many dancers are born with this Life Path and there is an attraction towards laughter, entertainment and the lighter side of life. They appear to be lucky people; they do make money easily. Something always seems to turn up for 3s. Eloquent and resilient, they are good hosts who enjoy being surrounded by people. They need to express their undoubted creativity in some way. Threes have sharp minds and love to party.

Negatively: they quickly become bored and restless. Although attracting money they cannot stop spending it. They have trouble coping alone and fear being by themselves. Endurance is not one of their strengths. They need to pace themselves more. This Life Path can burn itself out rushing around.

The 3's gift of providing laughter is shown by the comedian, Bill Cosby; creative entertainment of a different sort by the film director, Alfred Hitchcock; the 'life of the party' image could be attributed to the film actress, Jayne Mansfield and the writer F. Scott Fitzgerald.

LIFE PATH 4: THE BUILDER

Direction: to build a life on solid foundations.
Opportunities: to use self-discipline constructively.
Keywords: Practical. Realistic. Orthodox. Hard-working. Loyal. Honest. Narrow-minded. Dogmatic. Dull.

Fours are practical people who are not afraid of making an effort. They will endure restrictions to be able to accomplish what they want from life. Serious, mature, with an organized way of doing things, they enjoy working to a plan. They push themselves and can work long hours. Life for them gets easier as they mature. The word 'foursquare', meaning in a solidly-based and steady way, describes their lives. They are constructive and like to build solid foundations. There is often an ability to work with their hands. They are dependable people, loyal and sincere. They like to *see* results. Security is important; they are unlikely to spend all of their money. Orthodox thinkers who dislike diverging from their plans, they can be slow making decisions. Always busy, laziness is not a natural state. When they feel secure they will take a risk, but not before. Life for them has to have a solid foundation.

Negatively: they are workaholics, never knowing when to rest. Early life can be difficult. An original approach to a problem can scare them. They fear the new. At times their thinking becomes rigid and dogmatic.

Life Path 4 has featured among British Prime Ministers of late: Margaret Thatcher, Harold Wilson and John Major all being 4s. The actors Clint Eastwood and Arnold Schwarzenegger show the conventional strength of the 4 persona.

LIFE PATH 5: THE COMMUNICATOR

Direction: to learn to seek freedom.
Opportunities: to communicate and create change.

Keywords: Communicator. Freedom-seeker. Versatile. Adaptable. Sexual. Quick-thinking. Analytical. Progressive. Procrastinating. Love of pleasure. Changing too often.

Fives need to be free and will react quickly if they feel they are being manipulated. A love of change, progression and anything new typifies this number. Fives adapt instantly when conditions change. They are multi-talented and need to use their versatility. Five is the number of the senses and these people radiate an unconscious sexual magnetism. They have an exciting and young attitude to life. This is a physical number with a liking for competitive situations. They work well under stress. They do not possess 'team spirit' but hide this from others. Fives are popular with both sexes and can communicate to all types of people. They are brilliant sales people; mentally quick and eloquent. They will seek a faster way to do things. With a love of travel they can easily live out of a suitcase. Curious about others, they do not miss much. Shrewd and analytical, they see other people as they are and have no trouble accepting them like that. They want to succeed and dislike failing but find it hard to accept help. Always good-humoured, they can motivate others.

Negatively: they are self-indulgent and lack patience. They can, when unbalanced, indulge themselves in the 'sex, drugs and drink' life-style. They take too many risks and are frequently change jobs or become so absorbed in a career or project, emotionally or mentally, they find it impossible to let go and change.

The 5's natural sexuality and avant-garde approach can be seen in Marlon Brando (acting); Mick Jagger (singing); Andre Agassi (tennis); and Rudolf Nureyev (dancing by leaping to freedom); the darker side of 5's popularity in Adolf Hitler.

LIFE PATH 6: THE TEACHER

Direction: to learn the joys of responsibility.
Opportunities: to be creative and create harmony.
Keywords: Harmonious. Creative. Well-balanced. Responsible. Just. Advisor. Fair. Meddlesome. Anxious.

Sixes need a well-balanced life. They constantly seek harmony and appreciate pleasant and beautiful surroundings. They enjoy working in partnerships and function well as part of a team. They are responsible people who take positions of trust seriously. During their lives responsibility is often thrust upon them. They dislike unfairness and love fair play. Extremely loyal, similar to 4 in this respect, they make friends for life. This is a domestic number, there is a love of the home ever present. They need a peaceful home life and feel unbalanced when it is not there. There is great creativity contained in 6; a love of the arts; the voice is often used creatively. Sixes can teach. They need to balance their lives and achieve a state of perfect harmony.

Negatively: they think they know what their friends should do – and tell them so. They interfere and meddle. Chauvinism (of either sex) can be present. Over-eating can be a problem. Too conventional and moralistic, they fail to see others' points of view. They worry themselves stupid over minor matters.

The creativeness of this responsible number is shown in the Life Paths of the actresses Meryl Streep, Vanessa Redgrave and Glenda Jackson.

LIFE PATH 7: THE INDIVIDUALIST

Direction: to learn by one's own experience.
Opportunities: to use knowledge and wisdom.
Keywords: Individual. Intuitional. Deep-thinker. Analytical. Mysterious. Spiritual. Perfectionist. Procrastinator. Will not accept advice.

Sevens need to spend some time each day by themselves. Without a small amount of solitude they find it difficult to perform to their best capabilities. Their talents are fitted for some sort of specialist capacity. They are not team people. They work best alone. Achievements often occur in a surprising way and are not what was originally sought after. Sevens have both intuitional and analytical skills but they can distrust their intuition. They prefer to work at their own pace and dislike being hurried. Perfectionists, they appear to procrastinate when they are simply waiting for conditions to become perfect to act. They plan secretively over a long period then strike with devastating suddenness. This Life Path is thought to dream in colour more than any other. They dislike being ordered around and take direction badly. Secretive, with deep emotions not shown willingly, they have the ability to help or heal. At heart 'a rebel', 7s are attracted to unusual or new spiritual beliefs or religions. Curiously, for a number with such spiritual potential they can be attracted to atheism. And, surprisingly for such a solitary number – they perform well in public.

Negatively: they appear cold and arrogant, especially on first meeting. Some 7s hide from others by talking continually. They dislike physical work. They make life hard for themselves by never listening to advice. Day-dreaming replaces life.

Two individual 7s, female icons of their times, are Sixties' model, Jean Shrimpton, and Diana, Princess of Wales. Great political figures include President John F. Kennedy, Nikita Khrushchev, Sir Winston Churchill and Václav Havel.

LIFE PATH 8: THE GOAL-SETTER

Direction: to learn to set goals.
Opportunities: to become independent.
Keywords: Ambitious. Powerful. Organized. Philanthropist. Dependable. Independent. Materialistic. Greedy. Ruthless.

An enjoyment of the battle and a struggle for power is enacted out in this Life Path. Eights are strong, tough, and can, if needed, be ruthless. They are dynamic and depend on themselves. They dislike being in the position of the dependent and striving for independence is important. Ambitious, with a need to balance the material with the spiritual, they set themselves goals throughout their lives. This is a powerful and confident number working for its rewards slowly. Busy and excellent organizers, their careers are usually more important than their home lives. This is a number of extremes: success or failure. They like to look good and appearance is important. They easily intimidate others. Sporting or athletic ability is often found. When well-balanced they are philanthropists and enjoy helping other people; having helped, they prefer to see others look after themselves. This number functions well in the business world where its self-reliance and power can shine. It does not always have an easy life. It usually has to work for its success.

Negatively: they get frustrated easily. They can neglect to show affection to loved ones and are not seen at their best in domestic situations. When materially greedy and over-ambitious, they start to appear unlucky.

A large roster of powerful personalities shows the self-confidence of the 8: Elizabeth Taylor, Joan Collins, Nancy Reagan, Barbra Streisand, Liza Minelli, Ginger Rogers, Jane Fonda, and amongst politicians, Saddam Hussein.

LIFE PATH 9: THE HUMANITARIAN

Direction: to learn how to show compassion.
Opportunities: to develop idealism and creativity.
Keywords: Compassionate. Humanitarian. Idealistic. Romantic. Dramatic. Creative. Magnetic. Unfocused. Temperamental.

Nines' opportunities are unlimited; this is because 9 is the only number that contains all numbers within it. Idealistic, 9s want to change the world, they desire to make life better for everyone. This is a broad-minded, tolerant and unconventional Life Path. Nines are charismatic and creative individuals. The dramatic power of the artist is present here. They make fine leaders of movements, cults, or religions and easily understand the need for religion in everyday life. A love of travel is present. They are emotional and loving people with the gift of showing compassion. They prefer to deal with the large problems of life rather than the small. There can be dramatic endings at times in their lives. They are not particularly good at financial matters, but materialism does not interest them much. They have many friends – other people are fascinated by the magnetic attraction of this number. Intense

18

and impatient, they are well suited to a life spent in the arts or the humanities. Psychic ability is often present.

Negatively: they can be impatient and temperamental. They need to control their tempers. More practicality is needed, plus attention to detail. They are not good judges of character and may be manipulated. They can sacrifice themselves needlessly.

The humanity of 9 is seen in Mahatma Gandhi; the artist in Shirley Maclaine and Brigitte Bardot, both in later life devoting themselves to humanitarian movements: Maclaine to the New Age, Bardot to the care of animals.

3 · THE BIRTHCHART

I've had more trouble with myself than anyone else I know.
                                                    Dwight L. Moody

The Life Path Number is always your most important number but the characteristics it represents will be affected by all the numbers in your birthdate. These numbers: your birth day, your birth month, your year of birth, will strengthen or weaken the effect of your Life Path Number; this is why two people with the same Life Path can be so different. We see this effect on the Birthchart:

3	6	9
2	5	8
1	4	7

Chart 1. The Birthchart

The Birthchart shows where each number is placed. Insert all your birthdate numbers in their appropriate squares. A zero in the date is ignored. No matter how often the same number occurs in your birthdate it goes into the same square. Someone born on 1.1.1911, for instance, would have five 1s in the 1 square, and one 9 in the 9 square.

This is how the composer Leonard Bernstein's birthdate would appear on his Birthchart – he was born on 25 August 1918:

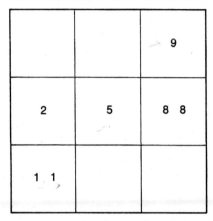

Chart 2. Leonard Bernstein's Birthchart

Everyone born before 2000 AD will have the number 1 on their Birthchart; everyone born in the new millennium will have a 2. These numbers represent the changing consciousness of the human race. As a generalization, babies born on or after 1.1.2000, and babies born on or before 31.12.1999, will differ fundamentally in their approach to life. The changing dates highlight the changing consciousness.

It is easy to see how the Birthchart can alter the effect of the Life Path Number. Here is a chart for someone born on 24.2.2000. He or she has a Life Path Number of 1.

This birthdate considerably softens the leadership qualities of the 1 Life Path. The Life Path would still be the most important number, but the cooperating influence of the three 2s would always be apparent.

The amount of numbers in each square and the missing

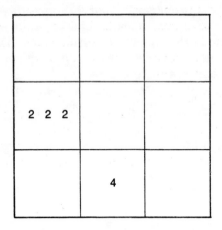

Chart 3. Birthchart: Date 24.2.2000

numbers on the chart are always considered alongside the influence of the Life Path Number. You may find the listed negative characteristics do not apply, but earlier in life they did. Thus your Birthchart shows how you have grown and developed.

BIRTHCHART 1s

One 1: They express themselves easily in public, through speaking or writing. In private they need to be more open with their emotions. Strong and self-reliant. They are inclined to talk quickly.

Two 1s: The ability to express themselves well at all times. In control of situations in a well-balanced way. This is an effective position for work in the business or entertainment worlds.

Three 1s: Great expressive ability, usually with the written word. Sometimes too much talent and the person appears hyperactive. This can be the sign of the chatterbox. They are usually happy people, but stubborn.

Four 1s and more: The potential for real achievement. Frustration develops if their lives do not offer possibilities for using their powers of expression or their ability to lead. They push themselves too hard and can be careless over their choice of food – under- or over-eating. If they allow themselves time to rest, high achievement is possible.

1 is missing: This will only occur in some charts after the last day of 1999. People with the 1 missing will need to develop the qualities of self-reliance and determination. They will need to be more willing to take the initiative and not allow others to take them for granted. They will need to assert their individuality.

BIRTHCHART 2s

One 2: Perceptive people. They form accurate assessments of others. Emotionally sensitive, often feeling uncomfortable in a competitive environment, preferring to work at their own more peaceful pace.

Two 2s: Awareness is heightened but they may not always heed their intuition. Inclined to mix with the wrong people sometimes. Usually their lives are well-balanced. They must beware of being overly sensitive.

Three 2s or more: Musical ability is often present. Emotional people, sensitive to others, but the need to protect their vulnerability can make them react in a cool or self-absorbed way. A hardness is shown which is foreign to their nature. They can be unwilling to take action and when forced to do so, over-react.

2 is missing: A need to appreciate and consider other people. Intuition and sensitivity can be distrusted. More willingness to cooperate is needed.

BIRTHCHART 3s

One 3: Interesting, enthusiastic and witty people. A powerful imagination which can be used in their career. Creative and bright. They help their friends when they need help. There is a strength behind this number that its bright facade does not always choose to reveal.

Two 3s: A strong imagination which needs disciplining. There can be a dislike of practicality. A tendency to daydream. An unorthodox approach to life that may be misunderstood.

Three 3s or more: Exercise or sport can be beneficial for this combination, although they may not be interested in doing it. There is a strong accent on the mind and the imagination. They can daydream and neglect the present. Keeping a balance between the activity of the mind and that of the body will benefit them.

3 is missing: A need to be more imaginative, or a fear of, or difficulty in, expressing creativity. Mathematics is often a problem area.

BIRTHCHART 4s

One 4: This adds practicality to any chart. Organized, with the ability to work until the job is finished. Tenacious, loyal and dependable. Often ability with the hands: the craftsperson, the artisan, the painter, or talent for playing a musical instrument.

Two 4s: A need for neatness and tidiness. The ability to work long hours. They need to watch they do not become over-materialistic. Dexterity with the hands is marked.

Three 4s or more: A feeling of restriction may be felt. This is the sign of the workaholic. These people need to remember to rest. Again, wonderful ability with the hands is often present and needs to be used. They can get into a rut and find it difficult to break free.

4 is missing: Practicality needs to be applied to day-to-day affairs. There can be a dislike of dealing with mundane, boring tasks. Carelessness over details causes problems. Tasks may not always be finished.

BIRTHCHART 5s

One 5: Five is the most important number on the Birthchart. Being at the centre, it links all the other numbers. Strength and determination is marked. The 5 can motivate others. It needs freedom. There may be problems in the domestic life as it dislikes restriction.

Two 5s: Freedom becomes more important and may cause problems at home. Self-control and determination is strengthened. There is the possibility of over-confidence which can cause mistakes.

Three 5s or more: People with many 5s love to take risks in life – sometimes they get away with them. Sensuality is present although often there is an unawareness of this. Determined and dynamic, they live life in the fast lane.

5 is missing: Determination and the ability to push themselves is often absent. They need motivation from an outside source. There is uncertainty which direction to take. They are aware of many opportunities but do not know how to use them. They benefit from a partner who will push them into action; or a name that provides support.

BIRTHCHART 6s

One 6: Creative, with a desire for a peaceful domestic environment. A love of art or artistic pursuits is present. There can be creative use of the voice. They become upset if their home life is disturbed.

Two 6s: Usually, a good memory with a fondness for food. They need to use their creativity. As with a single 6, the home will be important. Worry and anxiety is experienced over minor matters.

Three 6s or more: A more relaxed attitude to the home and family is needed. There is enormous creative potential here but the likelihood is they will be distracted by domestic matters.

Anxiety is often experienced outside the home environment. They need to remember their loved ones have to make their own mistakes in life.

6 is missing: Not particularly domesticated. Their home life will not be the centre of their universe. An appreciation of beauty or art may need to be developed. As children they may have been over-sensitive towards one parent. Something may be missing from their domestic life.

BIRTHCHART 7s

One 7: Philosophical, with a need to see justice done. This is the most difficult number on the chart. They dislike being taught or told what to do. This can create many hard learning experiences and life will not appear easy. Physical expression is heightened.

Two 7s: A deep interest in the meaning of life. With any 7 on the chart, interest can develop – often late in life – in the metaphysical, spiritual or occult worlds. Life is not always easy for two 7s. They make it hard on themselves with the extreme stress they place on their individualism. They dislike accepting help.

Three 7s or more: This is sometimes seen as a sacrificial arrangement of numbers. Setbacks can be encountered. A great deal of inner knowledge is contained here, and though they make life hard for themselves – sometimes by their own actions – they philosophically accept the results and try again. They possess wisdom.

7 is missing: Often a reluctance to rely upon themselves. There may be a fear of loneliness and a distrust of anything metaphysical. They need proof. They are usually not over-fond of exercise.

BIRTHCHART 8s

One 8: Good at assessing the capabilities of others. They are excellent at organizing projects and coping with details. Tidy people. As children they can be restless. They have no problem attacking work but sometimes find difficulty in finishing it.

Two 8s: Extremely capable people. They are shrewd in assessing others and can be intimidating. Often successful in the business world. They welcome a certain amount of change in their lives as they have unbounded mental energy that needs to be used up. There can be a distrust of the metaphysical.

Three 8s or more: A fortunate combination for a business person if they can keep a balance between the material and the spiritual. The tendency is to become materially greedy, but if this is kept in check, a well-balanced person emerges with very good assessment of others. This can be used to advantage. Often restlessness occurs.

8 is missing: Organization is needed. Detailed work will be avoided. Laziness or carelessness with money can be apparent. Attention to mundane tasks is needed if all that is gained is not to be lost.

BIRTHCHART 9s

One 9: Idealism, an awareness of the world and its people as interrelated, is shown here. During the final 100 years before 2000 AD, the 9 is on everyone's Birthchart. It signifies a subconscious awareness of the potential effects of human achievement. It has promoted a more tolerant or broad-minded attitude to grow as the century has aged. Negatively: it has promoted aggression and war.

Two 9s: Mental activity is strong. There is dramatic and creative potential with these numbers. It is important to keep emotionalism in check. While the desire to help humanity is often felt, it is important to be aware of what is achievable in a practical sense.

Three 9s or more: These numbers show a powerful use of the intellect. A revolutionary fervour may be felt to right wrongs or find better ways of living. These people are not good judges of character and must beware of exploitation. A charismatic and explosive combination.

9 is missing: The dynamism of the 9 will be missing from some Birthcharts from the year 2000. While human achievements may not be so marked, the peace and cooperation the 2 will bring will compensate. Without 9, a broader view of life will need to be developed and an awareness of what can ultimately be achieved.

LINES ON THE BIRTHCHART

A series of three numbers on your Birthchart strengthens your character in some way, depending on what the numbers are. These numbers are called Full Number Planes, Arrows of Pythagoras, or Lines. These successive numbers can be vertical: 123; 456; 789; horizontal: 369; 258; 147; or diagonal: 159; 357. It does not matter how many numbers are in each square as long as all three squares have at least one number in them. You may have more than one Line. It is possible to have five (example: born 25.3.1978). Three or more Birthchart Lines shows a strong personality with the *possibility* of easy achievement. It does not show the *attainment* of material success nor spiritual fulfilment. In theory, these should both

		9 9
2	5	
1 1		7

Chart 4. President Kennedy's Birthchart

be easier to gain with three or more Lines. In practice, people with no number Lines, or many numbers missing, achieve a great deal. From early in life, they are more aware of what needs to be done.

Looking at Chart 4, the Birthchart of the late President John F. Kennedy (5.29.1917), we see he has one complete Line: 159. This is the Line of Determination.

Three successive missing numbers on your Birthchart highlights a weakness, an area that needs to be strengthened. The Birthchart of the writer Emily Brontë (30.7.1818) shows she has one Line of missing numbers: 456. This is the Line of Frustration.

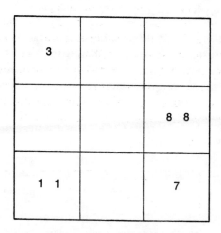

Chart 5. Emily Brontë's Birthchart

When there are two numbers on a Line, but a third number is missing, that Line is strengthened but not complete. Where two numbers on a Line are missing, it needs strengthening but is not completely weak.

COMPLETE NUMBER LINES

1–2–3 Line of the Planner: Good ability to make plans; to think before acting; to recognize the goals and the best way to reach them. Orderly, tidy, with business expertise. Drive, cooperation and the ability to mix with others.

4–5–6 *Line of the Will*: Whatever they dream, whatever they want, they will concentrate on to the exclusion of everything else. Extreme will-power. Ambitions desired as a child will not willingly be given up. They hold on to a single purpose in life.

7–8–9 *Line of Action*: Busy, powerful, with tremendous energy. Life will not stand still. While others plan and dream they will take action. Once decisions are made they will not procrastinate. Physical energy is high. Rest, fresh air and a healthy diet are important. Nervous headaches are associated with these active characteristics.

3–6–9 *Line of the Intellect*: Logical thinkers, usually with good memories and highly intelligent. They are creative thinkers. The mind is well-balanced and problems are solved easily and quickly. They can be impatient with others less bright.

2–5–8 *Line of Emotion*: Love, spirituality and sensitivity towards others is expressed in a well-balanced way. Artistic expression of the emotions is marked. There is usually performing ability. Love is important. They have deep emotional needs.

1–4–7 *Line of Physicality*: Good health and physical stamina are helped with this strong line. Ability with the hands is often present (either in a practical way or artistically). Too much emphasis can be placed on the career which is oddly balanced against a revolutionary outlook. A dynamic Line that often meets set-backs in life through restrictions set up by the 4 combined with the refusal to accept help of the 7.

1–5–9 *Line of Determination*: Determined to do many things well. All babies born in the 1950s had this Line, becoming the over-achievers of the Eighties. They can persist and bounce back from set-backs. They may cling to ideas or projects when the time is long past to let go.

3–5–7 *Line of Compassion*: Inner calm and an acceptance of the highs and lows in life mark these people. Towards others they are understanding and compassionate. There is often psychic ability present. A combination of joy and intuition describes them. Sorrows can occur, but they meet them with serene acceptance.

MISSING NUMBER LINES

1–2–3 cannot be a missing Line. But when two of these numbers *are* missing it shows a need to think before acting, a need to plan the life and its goals in a more constructive way.

4–5–6 *Line of Frustration*: Sometimes called the Saturn Line. Family life can present problems. There can be a reluctance to acknowledge what is truly desired. A hesitancy to accept their own needs. Too much will be expected from others. They need to feel free to act without approval.

7–8–9 *Line of Inertia*: They prefer to contemplate and perfect their ideas before acting. Procrastination may be seen by others but this is inaccurate. They need to be willing to take action rather than think about it.

3–6–9 *Line of Eccentricity*: Unconventional thinkers. They will not always apply logical thought to situations and may have difficulty using their creativity. They need to welcome the artistic and inspired into their lives.

2–5–8 *Line of Sensitivity*: Over-sensitive to the opinions of others. As children there can be a lack of self-confidence, an inferiority complex. Introverted and not usually comfortable in large groups, they need to like themselves more.

1–4–7 *Line of Illusion*: Practicality and materialism will be of little concern. A need to take more dynamic action in life. Physical stamina may be weak and they may dislike being alone. Life can be lived in a rut and a less conforming spirit will need to be developed.

1–5–9 *Line of Resignation*: Originality, motivation and determination may be lacking. When containing full numbers this

Line is exciting and strengthening; when missing, a lack of purpose and resignation prevails. They need to not always follow others.

3–5–7 Line of the Sceptic: This Line has two meanings. The first: people who demand proof, suspicious of anything metaphysical (such as this book) and orthodox in their beliefs. The second meaning appears more frequently today: open-minded, welcoming new ideas and beliefs – the opposite of the first. A Line that appears to offer a choice. Migraines and nervous complaints are associated with it.

The Birthchart, its numbers and Lines, must always be combined and analysed with your knowledge of your Life Path Number. The two are inseparable.

4 · THE BIRTHDAY AND GOAL NUMBERS

> All things which can be known have number, for it is not possible that without number anything can be either conceived or known.
>
> Philolaus

Your Birthday Number is the number of your day of birth. It represents how you think and act when alone. It has an effect on your first name. It shows how you interact in everyday situations. It influences your Life Path but is not as important.

It does not represent your direction or opportunities or show your *main* talents. It reveals abilities and strengths you are comfortable with. There should be no difficulty recognizing yourself and your actions from this number. Friends may recognize you from your Birthday Number easier than they do from your Life Path.

It *is* an important number, for the numbers in your birthdate are superseded only by the Life Path. Contrarily, in Indian numerology the Birthday Number is often of paramount importance.

It is your second *lucky* number – second in strength to the Life Path, this time regarding good fortune.

Research comparing professions with birthdays has been carried out by the Australian numerologist, Robin Stein, detailed in her book, *Your Child's Numerology*. A recommended read.

The following brief description of your birthday is added to the information obtained from your Life Path and Birthchart. Birthdays 1 to 31 are listed. Later, we will use fadic addition on this number. Negative and positive aspects are included, the positive being stronger.

BIRTHDAYS

1st: Leadership and ego. A dislike of taking orders from others. Self-employment attracts, or any original line of work. A need to stand alone. Determined, courageous and self-confident. There can be a disinclination to show affection.
Born this day: Boris Yeltsin, J.D. Salinger.

2nd: Cooperative and hesitant. Loving, sensitive and intuitive. Can work with or for others. Likes partnership or teamwork. Kindness is a positive trait. Easily becomes discouraged or depressed.
Born this day: Mahatma Gandhi, Dr Benjamin Spock.

3rd: Happy and jealous. Gregarious, popular and sociable. Brings laughter and joy to any group. A natural wit. Often a hidden fear of loneliness. Can be restless. Fun to be with but easily bored.
Born this day: Gore Vidal, Gertrude Stein.

4th: Stable but gets into a rut. A practical hard worker. Stability is important. A need to build the life on secure foundations. A loyal, patient and honest friend. Attracted to the orthodox and uncomfortable in changing conditions. A good day for politicians and doctors.
Born this day: Dr Thomas Barnardo, Francisco Franco.

5th: Adventurous and self-indulgent. Enthusiastic and versatile. Forever seeking the 'new'. Progressive with an unconscious sexuality. A love of travel and change. A surprisingly good birthdate for politicians.

Born this day: William S. Burroughs, Raquel Welch.

6th: Responsible and anxious. Many teachers are born on this day. Concerned with justice. Reliable friends. Creative people with a need to live in harmony. A strong love for their family over whom they worry unnecessarily.
Born this day: Sigmund Freud, Elizabeth Barrett Browning.

7th: Individualistic but procrastinating. Silent and secretive. A need for solitude. Seven keeps itself well-balanced by spending time alone. Analytical and intuitive, often absorbed in thought and attracted to the spiritual or occult.
Born this day: Saint Bernadette, Billy Graham.

8th: Goal-setting and greedy. Usually ambitious. Seeking independence. Good organizational ability. Many writers and scientists are born on this day. A balance needed between the career and the home, usually the career dominates.
Born this day: Katharine Hepburn, Dr Christiaan Barnard.

9th: Compassionate and quick-tempered. A love for humanity. Broadminded. Emotional and dramatic. Creative and idealistic with serious aims. Practicality often needed.
Born this day: Simone de Beauvoir, Glenda Jackson.

10th: Original and self-centred. Similar to the 1st. Self-confident and self-assured. Many actors born under this number. Single minded. Great energy. Arrogance needs to be watched.
Born this day: Fred Astaire, Marcel Proust.

11th: Inspired and impractical. Similar to the 2nd. Ability to cooperate. Not over-concerned about financial matters. Music and rhythm attracts. Daydreaming has to be curbed. Leadership ability preferably with help from a strong partner. A charismatic day. Many artists born here.
Born this day: Irving Berlin, Martha Graham.

12th: Creative but sacrificial. Similar to the 3rd. Bringing many singers and musicians into the world. Popular and gregarious with the ability to get things done. Ups and downs in life. Periods of sacrifice but always the ability to cope.
Born this day: Frank Sinatra, Maria Callas.

13th: Achieving and self-destructive. Similar to the 4th. A practical number with the ability to create change on a large scale. Hard working. Needing to listen more to the opinions of others. More vulnerable and emotional than they appear. A number of surprises.
Born this day: Fidel Castro, Arnold Schoenberg.

14th: Analytical but pleasure-seeking. Similar to the 5th. Curious, with a sybaritic approach to life. Attractive and sensual people – attracting hangers-on. When self-disciplined much can be accomplished, especially along progressive lines. Travel attracts.
Born this day: Cecil Beaton, Albert Einstein.

15th: Just but meddlesome. Similar to the 6th. Responsible with a love of fair play. Home life is important but they dislike spending all their time there. Original people with a love of beauty. Vanity has to be watched. They learn new ways easily.
Born this day: Florence Nightingale, Martin Luther King.

16th: Intuitive and nervous. Similar to the 7th. Needing solitude. Self-critical, setting themselves high standards. A dislike of interference in their affairs. Religion, medicine and writing are careers this number is often attracted to. They need to relax.
Born this day: Noel Coward, Oscar Wilde.

17th: Physical and reckless. Similar to the 8th. Traditionally considered a good number for financial matters, although life is often success or failure for 17. There is usually physical ability. Sportspeople and dancers are often born under this number.
Born this day: Rudolf Nureyev, Rita Hayworth.

18th: Powerful but materialistic. Similar to the 9th. Broad-minded with wide-ranging interests. Friction is felt between acting for the good of others or putting themselves first. Leadership is often given to them – even when not seeking it.
Born this day: Greta Garbo, Lucrezia Borgia.

19th: Independent but arrogant. Similar to the 1st. Tackle life in an original way. They dislike receiving advice but always

consider the needs of others. Moods can be up one minute, down the next. Emotional people.
Born this day: Coco Chanel, Jean Genet.

20th: Kind but anxious. Similar to the 2nd. Loving people. They dislike taking action without the approval of others. Good at detailed work. Musical and artistic. They easily become pessimistic.
Born this day: Sergei Rachmaninov, Henrik Ibsen.

21st: Lucky but extravagant. Similar to the 3rd. Considered a 'lucky' number. Attractive and cheerful, often in the right place at the right time, and usually the centre of attention. A need to concentrate and not fritter away opportunities.
Born this day: Florenz Ziegfeld, Robin Williams.

22nd: Masterful and dominating. Similar to the 4th. Considered the most powerful day to be born on. Natural leaders, with a genuine ability to construct their own lives. Nervous tension needs watching. Twenty-twos rarely doubt their instincts which are usually accurate.
Born this day: Mrs Rose Kennedy, D.W. Griffith.

23rd: Freedom-seeking but over-indulgent. Similar to the 5th. Loving change, freedom and pleasure. This number can hesitate to express its real emotions. Anything new appeals. An interesting, if untameable, personality.
Born this day: Joan Crawford, Joan Collins.

24th: Artistic and over-serious. Similar to the 6th. The decorative arts attract. The home is an important place. Creativity is valued. They are trustworthy, loyal and friendly.
Born this day: Henri de Toulouse-Lautrec, Barbra Streisand.

25th: A perfectionist but secretive. Similar to the 7th. Freedom-seeking, making decisions slowly. Calm, with intuitive insight. Can appear shy at first. Able to keep secrets.
Born this day: Pablo Picasso, Virginia Woolf.

26th: Charismatic but over-stressed. Similar to the 8th. Dependable and well-organized. Revolutionary thinkers with financial ability and, surprisingly, a love of domesticity. A

balance is kept between home and career. If in business they often have artistic hobbies.
Born this day: Mao Tse-tung, Leo Trotsky.

27th: Humanitarian but impatient. Similar to the 9th. Independent with a calm manner. Hard to anger but intimidating when aroused. Religion or science often attracts. Travel is enjoyed. There is usually a vivid imagination.
Born this day: Confucius, Mother Teresa of Calcutta.

28th: Initiative shown but selfish. Similar to the 1st. Self-employment or leadership attracts, although this number succeeds best with a partner. A combination of determination, originality and perception. A strong will with the ability to mix with others.
Born this day: Jacqueline Onassis, Beatrix Potter.

29th: Protective but scattered. Similar to the 2nd. A sparkling, musical, inspiring personality. An emotional and dramatic life at times. They need to comfort others. Spiritual, with strong beliefs, sometimes allowing themselves to be manipulated.
Born this day: Oprah Winfrey, Michael Jackson.

30th: Popular and easily bored. Similar to the 3rd. Many friends and the centre of attention. Natural entertainers. A love of life is present. They possess a wit that is too insightful at times. Happy people – scattering their energy.
Born this day: Truman Capote, Sir Winston Churchill.

31st: Attractive but orthodox. Similar to the 4th. Practical and creative – a potent mix. An unusual combination of hard worker and the artist. Unselfish people with distinctive good taste. Intuition and practicality combined can cause stress.
Born this day: Anna Pavlova, Norman Mailer.

In conventional numerology fadic addition is used on your Birthday Number: this shows its true essence. If there are two digits in your number (as in 11, 23) add them together, continuing until a single digit is left. This is the same process we applied to find the Life Path Number.

From now on, when your Birthday Number is mentioned, it will be the fadic number that is referred to. The general traits of each Birthday Number are:

1. (or 10, 19 & 28) Leading. Original. Self-confident.
2. (or 11, 20 & 29) Cooperative. Friendly. Kind.
3. (or 12, 21 & 30) Creative. Self-expressive. Witty.
4. (or 13, 22 & 31) Practical. Self-disciplined. Hard working.
5. (or 14 & 23) Communicative. Freedom-seeking. Versatile.
6. (or 15 & 24) Responsible. Creative. Advisory.
7. (or 16 & 25) Intuitive. Analytical. Solitary.
8. (or 17 & 26) Ambitious. Goal-setting. Independent.
9. (or 18 & 27) Compassionate. Dramatic. Idealistic.

Sometimes, it is easier to use your Birthday characteristics than those of your Life Path. If the two numbers are the same number there is no problem; but if different, your Life Path always shows your true direction – your path to fulfilment. Following the Birthday and ignoring the Life Path will lead to frustration.

The Birthday adds talents and strengths to the Life Path. As the Life Path is always the most important, what you receive from your Birthday Number may help or hinder your Life Path talents.

If your Life Path and Birthday are different numbers, but both odd or both even, the combination is harmonious. You will be aware of the two sides of your personality but will not experience many inner problems. For instance: the actor Robert Redford has a 1 Life Path, and a 9 Birthday. His *important* trait would be that of the leader, the initiator, but he would also have the humanitarian qualities of the 9. Likewise, someone with the vitality of a 5 Life Path would be a calmer person with the effect of a 7 Birthday Number.

If you have one even and one odd number, there is a certain amount of conflict. The important point to remember is the Life Path is *the* track to follow in life. It is your most important number *always*. If the qualities of the Life Path are consciously cultivated, problems in life gradually ease.

THE GOAL NUMBER

There is another important number in your birthdate: the Goal Number. It represents what you can achieve – what your Life Path is leading you to. It is third in importance. Disregarding this 'goal' usually brings out the negative tendencies of the number. It is found by adding your Birthday Number and month of birth together, using fadic addition to reduce to a single digit.

For instance: Jacqueline Onassis was born on the 28th July – adding 28 (Birthday 1) and 7 (July) together, we get her Goal Number, which is 8.

Goal Number 1: The goal is leadership.
Goal Number 2: The goal is friendship.
Goal Number 3: The goal is to express creativity.
Goal Number 4: The goal is practical achievement.
Goal Number 5: The goal is freedom.
Goal Number 6: The goal is accepting responsibility.
Goal Number 7: The goal is wisdom and self-knowledge.
Goal Number 8: The goal is material success.
Goal Number 9: The goal is expressing universal love.

5 · THE VOWEL NUMBER

A name is a kind of face.

Thomas Fuller

Your name affects what you want, how other people see you, and most importantly what you do. To say a name has any effect appears to some a foolish statement. But if a word and its sounds can affect us – and all words do – this must also apply to your name. Your name is still a word.

Think how long parents spend selecting the *right* word for their child. A baby recognizes this word – its name – between one and two years old; its last name around the age of three. This name becomes a personal symbol. It feels inseparable from you. You hear it day after day. It influences your actions. The sounds of this personal symbol become a part of you.

The following names all sound different, regardless of which sex they are associated with: Sue, Caradoc, Charmaine, Bill. Each name has a special sound that affects the owner. Numerological analysis can show the effect of the name, but two people with the same name will always react towards it in an individual way.

The writer Bernard Spencer Le Gette in a book on the Hebrew system of numerology: *Numera*, gives an original illustration of how names affect us. He suggests imagining everyone was called by the first line of a song – instead of a name. Imagine if every day you responded to the carol: 'Silent night, holy night'; or would you become a different person if your name was, 'You're simply the best!'?

Unsung, our names are no different. We are just used to hearing them spoken. But their sounds and rhythms still affect us.

Your name is not inseparable from you as your birthdate is. It may feel so. But it is not. It has been chosen by you or your parents. It can always be changed; your birthdate cannot.

Married women in our society traditionally change their names. When married they take their husband's last name and can experience a change in attitude. The new name helps mould a different person. This can be for better or worse, but often creates a feeling of confusion as the new name is adjusted to. The man keeps his own name and changes less. This seems unfair.

The spoken name creates vibrational patterns that affect us. Our names become part of the energy field around us – our aura. In an excellent book that delves into word analysis, *Behind Numerology*, the author Shirley Blackwell Lawrence describes a machine, an 'eidophone', that can show how words when spoken form different vibrational patterns in the atmosphere that we cannot see. Beautiful sounding words form harmonious patterns; brutal or ugly words create haphazard formations. The machine proves that words or names affect the atmosphere. It offers proof of what we cannot see but often feel. The name that you hear and respond to every day affects you. F. Scott Fitzgerald once wrote, 'You can stroke people with words.' What effect does your name have?

The name you are known by is your *real* name. This name contains the sounds that affect you day in, day out. This name gives an accurate analysis. Your full birth certificate name is what you started life with. The name you are now called is what you have become.

If your name is hyphened like Mary-Jane, or spoken as one, as in Billy Ray, analyse this as one name, as long as Mary-Jane and not Mary is the name you are called. Include middle names and initials only if you *always* use them.

The full name you use is most important. The vowels show

what motivates you. The consonants affect how you see yourself when alone and the first impression your personality makes on others. The total number obtained from the vowels and consonants combined shows how you interact with other people.

Your name is affected by the numbers of your Life Path and Birthday and the pattern on your Birthchart. If the Birthchart pattern is strong – three or more Lines – the name will have slightly less effect than if the Birthchart is weak. A good name, one that compliments your Life Path, is an advantage and to be desired.

Your first name affects your personal affairs and has a strong influence on you when you are alone; your last name or surname usually represents family or inherited traits and, unless you are always addressed by it, will have less influence.

Your full name; first and last names (and for some middle) combined, influences your public persona and represents the 'total' you. This full or complete name contains your most important name numbers. It symbolizes you, to yourself and to others. It is this symbol we will analyse.

The letters of our alphabet are numbered. There is a natural progression from A to Z: A is 1 and Z is 26. In conventional numerology, fadic addition is used on all the letters of the alphabet that have double numbers: from 10 to 26 – from J to Z. This shows the essence of each letter. Using this we see that A(1), J(10), and S(19) are all represented by the number 1. This means that A, J and S have something in common, they are all related.

The following table shows the number for each letter:

1	2	3	4	5	6	7	8	9
A	B	C	D	E	F	G	H	I
J	K	L	M	N	O	P	Q	R
S	T	U	V	W	X	Y	Z	

We will now analyse the influence of your vowels. This vowel number has many names: Motivation, Soul Urge, Ambition, Heart's Desire, and others. We will simply call it the Vowel Number. It shows what is wanted from life, what is desired. In ancient times the vowel sounds were considered sacred. They are still the inner life of the name, hence they show the inner or hidden motivation. When a name is changed and the Vowel Number alters, the person concerned does not immediately start wanting something different; but over a period of time, as the vibrations of the new name take effect, the motivation will change. The Vowel Number is second in importance only to the number for the complete name.

The vowels are A, E, I, O and U. Some numerologists also use Y, some never, and some only if there is no other vowel in the name. It is suggested you use Y as a vowel only if there is no other vowel in the same syllable: in Ty, Y would be a vowel; in Sally, Y would be a vowel; in Rodney, Y would not be a vowel. You will probably find this guideline is correct. Unfortunately, Y is a confusing letter, and if you have it in your name, try calculating it both as a vowel and again as a consonant. You will recognize which way is right for you. The influence of Y means you can be motivated in two different ways.

Using the table on p.43, we place the numbers for each vowel above the letter in the name. We then use fadic addition (continuing to add all the numbers together until one single digit is left) and the final total is the Vowel Number. Here as an example is the name of the tennis player Andre Agassi. His Vowel Number is 8:

```
1       5    1   1       9      = 17, 1+7 = 8
A N D R E    A G A S S I
```

THE VOWEL NUMBERS

Vowel Number 1: Wanting to take the lead; they like to see their ideas and wishes promoted. They prefer to work alone and can enjoy self-employment. The original and unorthodox path is preferred. They seek independence. A sense of humour is retained and they are usually optimistic. They may disregard the wishes of others. Once they make a decision they will be impatient to begin. They want their own way.

Vowel Number 2: Wanting to cooperate and work easily with others. They may be reticent or shy about making the first move. Sometimes they prefer someone else to take the first step. They have no difficulty following. They prefer life at a slow and steady pace and dislike to be rushed. Twos are attracted to music and rhythm. They want peace and are uncomfortable in a highly competitive environment. They are sensitive to others' feelings. They wish to be inspired.

Vowel Number 3: Wanting to have fun. They desire pleasant conditions and a lively atmosphere. They are ambitious and need to use creativity in whatever they do. When work is finished they want to party and enjoy themselves. They like having people around and need constant stimulation otherwise they get bored. Threes are attracted to the glamour of life. Good at judging others' motives. They enjoy talking. At times they can be vain and jealous.

Vowel Number 4: Wanting an orderly and organized life. They have a practical view and distrust the unconventional. Stability and security are important. Fours are not afraid of hard work but can feel restricted and become stuck-in-a-rut. If they feel dull for a long time they dramatically alter their desires, but most of the time they abhor sudden change. Fours feel comfortable with set boundaries.

Vowel Number 5: Wanting freedom and an unrestricted lifestyle. They need to communicate with others and are always interested in new and progressive ideas. They like to try everything at least once. Fives are versatile and adapt instantly to changing circumstances. They change their interests when they have experienced something completely. Travel always appeals. Sex is usually important. Restless, they can over-indulge themselves in pleasure.

Vowel Number 6: Wanting to help and easily accepting responsibility. They need to see justice done and have a strong sense of right and wrong. They wish to see others behave as responsibly as themselves. A six needs a quiet and harmonious home life. They desire and want to give love. Creative ability needs to be used. Uncomfortable when living in less than perfect conditions. They seek perfection.

Vowel Number 7: Wanting time alone to think. They need to make up their own minds and dislike being told what to do. They analyse everything but also use intuition. They have a strong sense of their own individuality. Sevens like to keep their secrets to themselves. They have a love of nature – often the sea. If unable to spend time alone with their thoughts they feel unbalanced. They like to experience everything at first hand. Sevens dislike advice.

Vowel Number 8: Wanting to achieve their goals. They are ambitious with a powerful urge to succeed. They strive for independence. Logical and organized in their aims, they can take ruthless decisions. Eights have powerful desires and experience frustration and bafflement if they do not fulfil them. They blame themselves. They need to relax more. If personal needs are gratified they will then help others who are less fortunate.

Vowel Number 9: Wanting to see their ideals played out in life. Nines feel compassion for others. They are understanding, with a wide range of interests. They like to travel. Unfortunately, they can scatter their energy over too many projects. Nines are romantic and enjoy the drama of life. Life is experienced on a grand scale. They have creative desires they need to satisfy. Too trusting of others, they have a strong love of life.

The effect your Vowel Number has on you depends on the number of your Life Path. Should both numbers (Vowel and Life Path) be the same, there will be no conflict in what you want to get out of life. This is the best combination to have.

If the numbers are different there will be some conflict over what you desire. If both numbers are odd, or both even, this is not seriously conflicting; the numbers may have different needs but they are complimentary and support each other.

If one number is odd and the other even, there is conflict. Your Life Path will be bringing you opportunities that you do not want. Your Vowel Number will create dreams and desires that are incompatible with your abilities and talents. The Vowel Number only shows what motivates you, not what you actually do. When we later look at the complete name number you may find you act more in keeping with your Life Path. The Life Path always shows the right direction to guide your actions.

If your Vowel Number is the same as your Birthday Number, care should be taken to not place too much emphasis on your Birthday characteristics at the expense of your Life Path (this only applies to Birthdays and Life Paths that are different).

As you will have realized, the combinations on your chart combine to form a rich pattern of possibilities.

6 · THE CONSONANT NUMBER

It is only shallow people who do not judge by appearances.
Oscar Wilde

The consonants in your name, added together, show the image you project to strangers. This is the first impression you make. This consonant number may not represent what you want nor how you ultimately act but it shows how you present yourself when appearing in public. It influences how you see yourself when you are alone. You may be unaware of this. It is closer to the influence of the Birthday than the Life Path.

This number has many names: the Personality, the Inner Self, the Impression, the Latent or Quiescent Self and others. We will call it the Consonant Number. It is your public and private image.

To find it we use the alphabet table (see p.43). Place the appropriate number beneath each consonant in your name. Use fadic addition to reduce to a single digit. Here is an example:

```
W I N S T O N   C H U R C H I L L
5   5 1 2   5   3 8   9 3 8   3 3 = 55, 5+5 = 10, 1+0 = 1
```

Winston Churchill has a Consonant Number of 1.

The first impression given by the Consonant Number can differ from the motivation shown by the Vowel Number. For example:

```
5   9   1   5           1       6     = 27, 2+7 = 9
  E L I Z A B E T H      T A Y L O R
  3   8   2   2 8        2   7 3   9   = 44, 4+4 = 8
```

Elizabeth Taylor's Consonant Number (8) gives a powerful, worldly and ambitious image; the Vowel Number (9) shows the motivation of the humanitarian. The projected image is more ambitious than what is desired. Here, Y has been used as a consonant. Y as a vowel would still show a difference between the numbers.

Looking at the vowels and consonants in any name or word enables us to determine the motivation and image that is created, as in these two words:

```
    9   5    = 14, 1+ 4 = 5    1       6     = 7
  W R I T E R                A C T O R
  5 9   2   9  = 25, 2+5 = 7    3 2   9  = 14, 1+4 = 5
```

See how 'writer' has the curiosity and need to communicate of the 5 but gives a solitary or secretive first impression by consonants that add up to 7. 'Actor' is the reverse: a 5 Consonant Number gives an extrovert first impression, belying the secretive, individual desires of the 7 Vowel. Cities and countries, words and names, can all be analysed numerologically from their vowels and consonants.

A word spelt differently in another language (but using the same common alphabet, such as French, Italian) will show through its numbers the differing approaches of each culture. Names should be analysed using their own alphabet. The following name is not an accurate analysis as the original name is not written in English, but see how the Vowel and Consonant Numbers affect our perception:

```
  1       1         3     5 9   = 19, 1+9 = 10, 1+0 = 1
S A D D A M      H U S S E I N
1   4 4   4      8   1 1     5   = 28, 2+8 = 10, 1+0 = 1
```

THE CONSONANT NUMBERS

Consonant Number 1: The image is that of the leader. Ones stride onto the stage of life with initiative, determination and originality. They look like they can look after themselves. There is an air of self-reliance about them. They appear self-confident, even if they do not feel it. They sometimes make enemies with their enthusiasm to see their own plans followed through. They appear to be unlikely to work well in a team situation. Happy, often instantly popular, they appear to need no help.

Consonant Number 2: The image is that of the friendly cooperator. They cope well when diplomatic skills are needed. Tact and the ability to provide advice, comfort and help are displayed. Inspirational, but always in a quiet way. There can be a degree of shyness at first. They will not always make the first move. Negatively, they can appear sly. They are seen as easy and natural people who make good friends.

Consonant Number 3: The image is of a bright, witty and happy person. Creativity is marked. There is a love of life, an enthusiasm for having a good time. Mentally sharp. Able to bring laughter and joy to everyone. They appear restless and quickly get bored. Gregarious people who come alive at social events. The image is of someone who possesses abundant good luck.

Consonant Number 4: The image is of a person with organizational skills who acts in a practical way in a crisis. A hard worker who is emotionally stable and self-contained. They appear to have strong self-discipline. Good at detailed work, they easily handle boring everyday chores. An orthodox and conservative personality. They prefer the natural to the artificial, appearing predictable but solid.

Consonant Number 5: The image is one of versatility. They appear to have many talents, to be able to turn their hands, with instant adaptability, to almost anything. Quick in reactions with insight and enthusiasm. They appear progressive. They want to try anything new. Hard to pin down and forever seeking freedom. There is a sexual attractiveness often displayed on first meeting. They appear more promiscuous than they are. Others are never quite sure about them. A dazzling paradox.

Consonant Number 6: The image is one of creativity allied with a sense of responsibility. They appear harmonious and well-balanced. There is a love of beauty. They appear to work well as part of a team or would make a responsible partner. They look like they can teach. The home seems to be their place of happiness. Over-anxious at times. A doting parent.

Consonant Number 7: The image is one of coolness, independence and deep thinking. They are hard to get to know at first. Solitary and secretive, they give nothing away. An individual type of person. They will not accept advice and insist on going their own way. They appear arrogant although this is just a natural reserve. They are not afraid to make the first move, they just do not want to.

Consonant Number 8: The image is strong, self-assured and capable. There is a feeling of power behind what they do. They appear ambitious and determined to make a success of their lives. They are goal-oriented. Their lives do not always appear easy. There can be an undercurrent of struggle or ill luck. The extremes of success or failure can typify 8. They are survivors. Tenacious. Kind to others. Sometimes greedy and materialistic. They need to feel in control.

Consonant Number 9: The image is dramatic, romantic and idealistic. A love of people and a broad-minded approach to life. There is a charismatic quality to this number. They appear compassionate humanitarians with an unconventional approach. Independent and creative. A dynamic presence that attracts others to them. Energetic, with a quick, exploding bad temper. Life appears far from dull.

The Consonant Number is not as important as the Vowel Number. What you want from life will always have a stronger influence on you than how you may appear. Nevertheless, it is still an important number and you will need, as with the vowels, to judge its effect with your Life Path.

If it is the same as your Life Path, the first impression you give is likely to be how you really are. But this may not show what you ultimately do nor what you desire.

If your Consonant Number and Life Path are both odd or both even numbers, it is a harmonious combination. Your image is not in serious conflict with your birthdate. If one number is odd and the other even, the impression you give is different from your true self. You may appear to others as an unlikely candidate for the opportunities that come your way.

STRESS NUMBERS

The area of conflict between any two numbers can often be found in the Stress Number. It is useful to know but is not an important number and does not need to be noted down.

To find any Stress Number you subtract one number from the other. It can be used to show the main problems between your Life Path and Vowel, your Vowel and Consonant, or any two numbers. Two even or two odd numbers subtracted from each other will not manifest conflicts as easily as when one number is odd and the other even.

As an example: Jane Austen's Consonant number was 5, her Life Path was 3 (numbers suggesting communication, curiosity and creativity). Her Stress Number here was 2 (3−5 = 2). Although Life Path and Consonant are both odd − suggesting a harmonious combination − her Stress Number shows if problems arose it would have been over cooperating, sharing, being willing to follow, and so on. All qualities of 2.

Greta Garbo's Life Path was 6, her Consonant Number 9 (a combination of creativity). Her Stress Number here was 3. This shows a difficulty with her image of projecting fun, laughter and gregariousness. She may even at times have been unwilling to use her creativity. It highlights her famed statement: 'I want to be alone.'

The positive and negative characteristics of the two numbers used to find the Stress Number are always more important. The Stress Number provides additional information.

MEANING OF STRESS NUMBERS

0: No stress number. This only occurs when both numbers are of the same value. A zero denotes little stress. Any difficulties that arise will be found in the negative aspects of the number involved.

1: Stress is shown over taking the initiative, taking the lead, being willing to forge ahead in an original way. There can be hesitancy to start anything new. A lack of ambition or dependency on others. Courage is sometimes lacking.

2: Stress is shown over being able to cooperate with others. There can be inability to show sensitivity or a dislike of displaying affection. Unable to follow directions. A dislike of sharing. A peaceful atmosphere can be difficult to maintain.

3: Stress is shown by taking life too seriously. Self-expression is difficult. Discomfort is felt in crowds, an inability to socialize. Enjoyment and pleasure are problem areas. A refusal sometimes to use creative talents.

4: Stress is shown over the need to consider the practical side of life. A refusal to lay down constructive plans for the future. A dislike of hard work or repetitive tasks is a problem. There is a lack of patience or tenacity.

5: Stress is shown over adaptability. An unwillingness to accept change or try anything new. There is a fear of freedom. A preference for staying put. Sexual needs may be ignored. An unwillingness to mix with others is felt. Competition is disliked.

6: Stress is shown related to the home. A dislike of accepting responsibility. Domestic life is a problem area. Creative pursuits may be cast aside. There is a lack of balance. Life feels uneven. It is difficult to not become over-anxious.

7: Stress is shown when left alone; a fear of loneliness or a dislike of working by oneself. There is a fear of psychoanalysis; a dislike of probing inner motives. Spiritual faith can be doubted. Learning by personal experience is avoided.

8: Stress is shown over career issues or matters of independence. Organizational skills can be lacking. Self-confidence is weak. A disinclination to exert power in any situation. A feeling of confusion. Showing ambition is deemed unhealthy. There is inability to choose a definite goal in life.

7 · THE NAME AND POWER NUMBERS

Names and natures do often agree.

John Clarke

Numerologists use many different names for the number of the name: Expression, Destiny, Character and others. For simplicity, we will call it the Name Number. It represents the complete name you are known by (first – sometimes middle – and last names combined). The total of all your letters.

It is the most important number found in your name; the most important number you have control of. You have power or control over it because you can change it. Many people do this unconsciously when they respond to a nickname. Women in Western society often do this on marriage.

The Name Number represents what you do – not what you *want* and not what you *think* you do. It shows how you interact with other people. In this sense it has an effect on the situations you attract but this influence is small compared to the opportunities the Life Path brings. Your Life Path represents your talents and the opportunities you attract; your Name Number influences what you do or how you interact with other people.

The Bible has many references to names: in Proverbs we

read, 'A good name is rather to be had than great riches'; in Samuel: 'As his name is, so is he'; and there is an old English proverb that states, 'A good name keeps its lustre in the dark.'

Your name acts as a symbol to strangers who have never met you. It forms an image of you, of what you look like, act like, are going to be, just from the sound and look of its letters.

In his novel, *Secret Lives*, the English writer E.F. Benson describes how Susan Leg sells her first novel. Her publisher begs her to use a pseudonym. 'People may ask, "What's in a name?" and my answer is, "A very great deal if you think of the right one."' Susan finds her name – and the book's title – in a dream. She wakes up '. . . with a crow of triumph, "Apples of Sodom by Rudolph da Vinci!"' The sound and look of words can paint a vivid image.

Numerologically, having the right name is important. There is an ancient belief that words that total the same number are connected. For instance: God, majestic, eminent, grand, zeal, smart, mega, success, influence and renown, all total the number 8. Words with the same number as your Name Number are related in some way. This little-investigated aspect of word analysis is examined by the authors Shirley Blackwell Lawrence, William Eisen and Henrietta Bernstein (see bibliography) and is a rewarding area to investigate.

If you have a good Name Number, it will help you through any difficult periods in your life – these periods or events are examined in Chapter 12.

Your Name Number is the fadic total of all the numbers in your name when added together; or the total of your Vowel and Consonant Numbers combined. It is the same thing. Here is how to calculate it:

```
  6   6         1   5    = 18, 1+8 = 9    Vowel: 9
C O C O     C H A N E L              Consonant: 7
  3   3       3 8   5    3 = 25, 2+5 = 7      16, 1+6 = 7 Name
```

THE NAME NUMBERS

Name Number 1: They interact with others in an original, assertive and self-aware way. They easily take the lead and

are not afraid of striding ahead into new fields alone. They prefer to take charge. Negatively: they experience difficulty in following orders. May act in a too determined manner and can be impatient.
Examples: Winston Churchill and Mahatma Gandhi.

Name Number 2: They interact with others in a friendly, diplomatic and cooperative manner. They attract and inspire people with their actions. There is an artistic need. They enjoy strong support. They cope well with details and patiently wait until the time is right to act. They dislike being rushed. Negatively: they may be indecisive and duplicitous.
Examples: Martin Luther King and Ronald Reagan.

Name Number 3: They interact with others in a vital and lively manner. They express themselves well and use wit and laughter to further their aims. They act in a gregarious manner and seek interaction socially. There is a need to use their creativity. They have a sense of fun. Negatively: they may get bored and have difficulty finishing what is started.
Examples: Maggie Smith and Lauren Bacall.

Name Number 4: They interact with others in a stable and unemotional manner. They follow a practical and logical approach with everything undertaken. They make certain, before acting, that their plans will work. They prefer an orthodox approach and tend to push themselves too hard, becoming workaholics. Negatively: they may get into a rut, becoming dull and rigid in their thinking.
Examples: Margaret Thatcher and Greta Garbo.

Name Number 5: They interact with others in an adaptable and versatile manner. They prefer to take a new or different approach to life. They dislike restrictions and will seek an element of freedom. They communicate well, having the ability to motivate others, and are usually popular. Negatively: they may change direction too often or get lost in pleasure seeking.
Examples: Elvis Presley and Liza Minelli.

Name Number 6: They interact with others in a loving and harmonious manner. They are unafraid of responsibility and

will offer a helping hand. They need a peaceful home life to function at their best. They need to use their creativity. Negatively: they may tell others what to do and interfere needlessly.
Examples: Brigitte Bardot and Bruce Springsteen.

Name Number 7: They interact with others in an individualistic way and will do their own thing. They ignore the easy or accepted way to do something. They need to prove to themselves that things work. They need time alone to think. A dislike of being taught by others. Negatively: they may daydream and defer taking action until conditions are perfect – which may be too late.
Examples: Michael Jackson and Arnold Schwarzenegger.

Name Number 8: They interact with others by setting goals to achieve. They act in an efficient and capable manner and have a businesslike approach. They act ambitiously, whether they want success or not. They consider those less fortunate but expect them to help themselves once help is given. Negatively: they may become greedy and power hungry.
Examples: Elizabeth Taylor and Warren Beatty.

Name Number 9: They interact with others by being broadminded, tolerant and showing compassion and understanding. They need to use their creativity. They prefer to act by considering the views of others. Their approach is idealistic. There is a liking for travel and a need for a wide panorama on which to act. Negatively: they may be impractical and spend all their money.
Examples: Judy Garland and James Dean.

Your Life Path and Name Number are important areas of your chart. If both numbers are the same there is little stress between what you do and the opportunities you attract. It is a fortunate combination to have. If both numbers are odd, or both even, it is still harmonious, although not perfect. One number odd and the other even is a difficult combination. You may not always take full advantage of the opportunities that come your way. As with your Vowel and Consonant Numbers, you can subtract one number from the other to find a probable area of stress.

POWER NUMBERS

Add your Life Path to your Name Number, using fadic addition, and you discover your Number of Power. This is sometimes called the Ultimate or Reality Number. It has a subtle effect on your chart. Its influence is always there in the background. It reveals what can be attained from the combined effect of your Life Path and Name.

As an example: Margaret Roberts had a 4 Life Path and a 9 Name Number, giving her a 4 Power Number. The hardworking aspect of her Life Path was combined with the idealism of the 9 Name. The Power 4 would have helped her towards constructive and practical achievements, although a 5 Stress Number would have indicated difficulties with freedom, communication, and a distrust of anything new.

When Margaret Roberts married and became Margaret Thatcher her Name Number changed to 4. Her Life Path and Name were now the same. Little stress between what she would do and her natural talents. An excellent combination. Her Power Number became 8, the natural number of the powerful tycoon or executive. This does not mean she would have been unable to have become a powerful political figure as Margaret Roberts, but the name change to Thatcher would have made the climb up the political greasy pole easier.

The Power Number shows the *easiest* position attained from the combined effect of your Name Number and Life Path.

Here is how to find it: the painter Pablo Picasso's Life Path was 8; his Name Number was 2: $8 + 2 = 10$, $1 + 0 = 1$. The Power Number was 1. Picasso had a strong but not easy Life Path, plus a 2 Name. The 2 would influence seeking a partner and foster artistic expression. His Power Number, a 1, helped achieve a position of originality.

A dislike of the Power Number is often found when there is disharmony between the Life Path and Name Number.

MEANING OF POWER NUMBERS

1: Life is influenced by originality, determination, and a brave and courageous ambition. The achievement is that of the leader, the originator, the inventor.

2: Life is influenced by the ability to work well with others, to collaborate, to use tact and diplomacy. The achievement is that of the inspired artist, the true friend, the peace-maker.

3: Life is influenced by using self-expression, bringing happiness, joy and laughter to others. The achievement is that of the creator, the entertainer, the joy-bringer.

4: Life is influenced by an ability to create a stable environment, being able to take a practical approach, laying strong foundations. The achievement is attained after steady progress: the constructive builder, the reliable person.

5: Life is influenced by communication, being at ease with others, seeking freedom and progress. The achievement is popularity, the person with many interests, the natural salesperson.

6: Life is influenced by taking responsibility, using creativity and bringing harmony to others. The achievement is that of the teacher, the artist, the protector.

7: Life is influenced by an ability to use solitude constructively, to use intuition and seek inner growth. The achievement is an awareness of spirituality, a philosophical outlook, a consciousness of individuality.

8: Life is influenced by projecting power, being efficient and working slowly towards material rewards. The achievement is that of the executive, the philanthropist, the material achiever.

9: Life is influenced by the ability to understand, to be broad-minded, to place a high value on showing compassion. The achievement is that of the dramatic artist, unlimited fulfilment and independence.

THE FIRST NAME NUMBER

You may want to analyse each of your names individually. This is advisable. Your complete name – as in your Name Number – is still your most important number, followed by your Vowel and Consonant Numbers. But your first name, in particular, has a definite effect on your personal life.

The First Name Number is sometimes called the Key, or the Core. It is found by adding, fadically, all the numbers in the first name together. It is affected by your Birthday Number. Whatever your Birthday Number is, it is better to have a First Name Number that is different, otherwise your Birthday characteristics risk being strengthened instead of your Life Path.

If your Life Path and Birthday are the same number, it is still better to have a different First Name Number. Traditionally, the first name is the 'key' to open the door to life; if the Birthday, the 'lock', is the same, you will not be able to open the door yourself and will need the assistance of others.

Numbers are traditionally associated with the four elements. It is thought better, by some numerologists, *not* to have the Birthday and First Name from the same number group. The groups are:

> Fire: 1 3 9   Air: 5 6
> Earth: 4 6 8   Water: 2 7

The number 6 can be in two groups. For characteristics of your First Name, consult the Name Numbers in this chapter. The Vowel and Consonant Numbers of your First Name can be analysed in the same way as for your complete name but applied on a more private or personal level.

Your last name usually shows inherited influences of your family. For most people nowadays their first name will be more important.

8 · THE ALPHABET

I often think how much easier life would have been for me and how much time I should have saved if I had known the alphabet.

W. Somerset Maugham

The first letter of a word dominates the letters that follow it. Think of: action, assert, autocrat, achieve, ambition; or: royal, regal, reign, renown, radiant and rich. The first letter of your name has a similar effect; when spoken it colours all its following letters. It is often called the Cornerstone. For simplicity, we will call it the First Letter.

It shows you your materialistic attitude and your *thinking* reaction to the world around you. It is not always listened to. It is not always acted upon. It has a subtle effect on your Name and First Name Numbers.

The first vowel in your name (A, E, I, O, U or Y) reveals your first emotional reaction. Its sound is believed to echo the soul of a name or word. If your First Vowel is also your First Letter, you may have difficulty making decisions – your emotional and mental reactions may be confused.

All the vowels in your name influence your emotions and needs. All the consonants influence your material thinking and hence your chosen outward appearance. Your First Letter is your most important letter.

The Last Letter (often called the Capstone) influences how

you conclude your affairs; the Middle Letter (sometimes called the Keystone) – this only occurs in names with an odd number of letters – highlights what may at times be a compulsion or obsession or an imbalance of energy. A mental note, only, needs to be made of your Middle and Last Letters; they are not as important as your First Letter and First Vowel. As an example:

$$\begin{array}{cccc} & 5 & & \\ C & H & E & R \\ 3 & 8 & & 9 \end{array}$$

The First Letter is C(3), showing the first mental reaction to be creative, bright and not taking things too seriously. The First Vowel is E(5), showing the first emotional reaction will be to communicate and seek to change things or possibly to seek freedom from restrictions. The Last Letter is R(9); matters would finally be dealt with in a responsive but powerful way. There is no Middle Letter. Notice how these three letters harmonize – they are all odd numbers. The letters need to be considered beside the Vowel, Consonant and Name Numbers – here they are mostly harmonious.

The Alphabet

A (1) A MENTAL LETTER

It is assertive and aggressive and thrusts its views into the world. This is seen in its shape – pushing upwards. The leader, with original ideas and ambitious plans behind it. There is an assurance about A. It has a quick temper and prefers activity to sitting still.

As First Letter: encourages leadership.

As First Vowel: acts assertively in emotional matters. There is a dislike of interference. It will not accept advice.

B (2) AN EMOTIONAL LETTER

It is introverted – two parts of the letter are enclosed, indicating shyness at times. It works well in partnership or as a

member of a team. It cooperates with others. It is sensitive and prefers to improve rather than initiate. There is an appreciation of beauty and the arts. It is helpful for expressing musicality and can deal with details. It may need outside motivation.
As First Letter: encourages cooperation.

C (3) AN INTUITIVE LETTER

It can express itself well and is outgoing and gregarious – notice how C is open on one side. It gives attention and gets it back. A creative letter with a degree of restlessness. Easily thrown off balance. It performs well before the public. is loving and needs to show it.
As First Letter: encourages creativity.

D (4) A PHYSICAL LETTER

Brings practicality, patience and efficiency to life. It works long and hard for what it wants. Must avoid getting stuck-in-a-rut – see its enclosed shape. It promotes orthodox thinking. Has the ability to lay down plans that work. Brings a pragmatic view to life.
As First Letter: encourages practicality.

E (5) A PHYSICAL LETTER

Encourages a versatile and adaptable approach. Restless, with a love of travel. It seeks freedom. This is a popular letter. It is open at the side showing ability to communicate but its lines are straight so it is direct in its approach. No beating around the bush. Sparkling and effervescent.
As First Letter: encourages communication.
As First Vowel: the emotional reaction is quick. If life is boring it changes its interests.

F (6) AN INTUITIVE LETTER

Brings a need to achieve harmony and balance in life. Not as secure as it appears and sometimes ignores practicalities.

Friendly and creative – often using the voice. Is responsible. It needs creative fulfilment in life and is drawn towards the performing arts.

As First Letter: encourages fun and friendship.

G (7) A MENTAL LETTER

Has the ability to communicate or withdraw into itself. Often prefers solitude. This is an enigmatic letter with creative potential. It works hard for what it believes in and encourages spirituality. It can be obstinate.

As First Letter: encourages self-reliance.

H (8) A MENTAL LETTER

H is materially powerful. It enjoys climbing the ladder of success (look at its shape). It works methodically towards what it wants and has financial acumen. Independent, often desiring social success. Open to new situations and aware of spiritual needs.

As First Letter: encourages financial abilities.

I (9) AN EMOTIONAL LETTER

Emotional and independent. It knows what it wants and dislikes interference. Idealistic and impractical. A romantic attitude to life. It can be over-dramatic. Impressionable and sensitive. I helps develop humanitarian instincts.

As First Letter: encourages idealism.

As First Vowel: it reacts in a romantic, idealistic, and impractical way.

J (10/1) A MENTAL LETTER

It has leadership qualities but is not as secure as it first appears and sometimes needs support. Look at its curved base, it can rock from side to side. It has a strong sense of self and prefers action to inaction. If it proceeds with caution, it achieves its ambitions. It can be inattentive.

As First Letter: encourages mental judgement.

K (11/2) AN INTUITIVE LETTER

Inspiration and inspired thought is given to the name with this letter. The ability to inspire others. It can cooperate but its idealism can sometimes be a problem. It does not like second best. It may create a nervous atmosphere around it.
As First Letter: encourages inspiration.

L (12/3) A MENTAL LETTER

Exerts a magnetic attraction. A loving, expressive letter that draws the public towards it. L is not serious in its attitude and prefers the lighter side of life. Critical when thwarted. It is more settled and secure than it appears and has planning ability. It is at ease in social gatherings.
As First Letter: encourages sociability.

M (13/4) A PHYSICAL LETTER

Can be extremely practical but craves love and excitement. It encourages a series of ups and downs in life and can be moody. Strong-willed, but will compromise rather than risk losing all. Conservative and orthodox with good ability to concentrate.
As First Letter: encourages integrity.

N (14/5) A MENTAL LETTER

Enjoys a life of change in which pleasure is not ignored. Sensual, preferring to be around others. Occasionally overdosing on the social scene. N helps with public recognition. When self-disciplined, it can attain what it wants. It tends to repeat mistakes.
As First Letter: encourages popularity.

O (15/6) AN EMOTIONAL LETTER

Represents the magic circle. O is self-contained, studious, and retains what it gains. A good financial letter. Will-power and self-discipline are strong. Like the sun – look at its shape – it attracts attention. It easily adapts to domestic changes.

As First Letter: encourages scholarship.

As First Vowel: the emotional response is responsible. It is aware of the spiritual in daily life. Can become emotionally fatigued.

P (16/7) A MENTAL LETTER

It has intellectual intensity and encourages deep thinking on many aspects of life. Surprising events can occur – conditions overturned or overthrown without warning. Encourages an interest in religion, metaphysics or the occult. It dislikes interference intensely.

As First Letter: encourages self-knowledge.

Q (17/8) AN INTUITIVE LETTER

Unusual, it adds eccentricity to the name. Financially acute, it has a different and distinctive way of living. It uses its intuition. Q enhances physical prowess. It can make mistakes in judgement but is still a good letter for anyone in business.

As First Letter: encourages unorthodoxy.

R (18/9) AN EMOTIONAL LETTER

A letter of power. Humanitarian instincts and a need for action and achievement. In the past, dubbed the 'growling' letter. Self-confident with materialistic and idealistic needs. Creative ventures helped. It can assist others but may be unwittingly used at times.

As First Letter: encourages determination.

S (19/1) AN EMOTIONAL LETTER

Many successes and failures with this letter, many twists and turns – look at its shape. S needs success and social esteem. It encourages ambition in any name. Not always secure and can become too self-absorbed. It can lead, but often prefers not to. Powerful and shrewd.

As First Letter: encourages ambition.

T (20/2) AN EMOTIONAL LETTER

The letter of the martyr – look at its shape, that of the cross. Loving, tactful and wishing to show friendship. It adds a degree of nervousness to the name. Not always comfortable in competitive situations and preferring to follow rather than lead. It has the ability to teach. It thrives on affection.

As First Letter: encourages trust.

U (21/3) AN INTUITIVE LETTER

A joyful and sociable letter. Open to express itself yet easily thrown off-balance. Its shape is open at the top with a base that can rock. Thriving on contact with people. It attracts good fortune but can carelessly lose it. A happy letter. Indecisive at times.

As First Letter: encourages gregariousness.

As First Vowel: the emotional response is loving and passionate, sometimes melodramatic.

V (22/4) AN INTUITIVE LETTER

One of the most powerful letters in the alphabet. It helps manifest far-reaching changes, mapping out its life by constructing dynamic plans that work. Nervous tension overpowers it at times. It can be ruthless.

As First Letter: encourages achievement.

W (23/5) A PHYSICAL LETTER

Look at its shape – like the waves of the sea. W has a life of ups and downs. A dizzyingly diverse life-style. Communication, adaptability and versatility are all here. It enjoys life to the full.

Pleasure and change are needed as much as work. A difficult letter to pin down, but always popular.
As First Letter: encourages versatility.

X (24/6) AN EMOTIONAL LETTER

A letter – like most letters at the end of the alphabet – of high voltage. X does not often occur in names. It gives sensuality and helps in public recognition. It can symbolize sacrificing oneself to a cause or belief. Underneath its glamour, it is exacting in its attention to detail. Needs a more settled life-style than it appears.
As First Letter: encourages personal magnetism.

Y (25/7) AN INTUITIVE LETTER

This letter faces many choices – look at the way it resembles a fork in a path. Spiritually inspired, it finds it hard to commit itself to a single cause of action. It helps in intellectual work. Works well alone. Psychic and intuitive ability is enhanced with Y. It promotes indecision.
As First Letter: encourages perception.
As First Vowel: emotionally indecisive but with strong intuition that can be used successfully.

Z (26/8) AN EMOTIONAL LETTER

Often compared to a flash of forked lightning – look at its design. This letter promotes recognition and fame. There is power and a love of luxury here. An interest in metaphysics or the occult can be present. A comfortable home-life is important. A good letter financially. Z is unconventional.
As First Letter: encourages power.

STARTERS, IMPROVERS, FINISHERS

The letters can be divided into three groups: the Starters, the Improvers, the Finishers. This provides additional information. Check where the majority of your letters lie.

The Starters: A E I K O R Z. These letters encourage the creation of projects, the ability to get things going. They are self-starters.

The Improvers: B F H J N P Q S T U W X Y. These letters encourage the ability to continue with projects; they promote ideas already started. They improve on what has been created. They can be indecisive at times.

The Finishers: C D G L M V. These letters encourage the completion of projects. They are constructive. They finish what they start.

As an example: the name John (as a first name), although beginning with J (1), is not a particularly strong name for starting projects – either from its letters or final numbers. It is more of an improver. Its potential for leadership would depend on the next name attached to it.

Letters are neither good nor bad. They are all different and influence people in differing ways.

9 · THE INTENSITY NUMBERS AND NAMECHART

It is with our passions as it is with fire and water, they are good servants but bad masters.

Roger L'Estrange

Within the name, a number repeated more times than any other is known as the Intensity Number. It shows a hidden desire. It is sometimes called the Ruling or Secret Passion. It can, if dominant, affect the characteristics of the Name, Vowel and Consonant Numbers.

Here is the name of a Hollywood star:

```
      1 5       5
    M A E     W E S T
    4         5   1 2
```

The 5 is repeated more times than any other number. Mae West would have had an Intensity Number of 5. The Name, Vowel and Consonant Numbers are still the most important; the Intensity adds further information. Mae West was noted for her witty remarks, especially relating to sex, and 5 is the number of sexual magnetism. Her Name Number was also 5 – further strengthened by this Intensity.

A single Intensity Number can have a strong effect. If you have two numbers present, the effect is weakened. Three or more Numbers of Intensity and the effect is diffused and little attention need be given to it.

When there is no Intensity Number, the name is well-balanced between the numbers it possesses.

THE INTENSITY NUMBERS

1: Intensifies the awareness of self. The will is strong and the name encourages assertiveness, originality, and self-confidence. It colours the Name Number with an ability to lead and a degree of initiative.

2: Intensifies a feeling of kinship with other people. Tact, diplomacy and cooperation are encouraged. It colours the Name Number with the ability to follow rather than lead. It adds a sense of rhythm and sensitivity to everything attempted.

3: Intensifies a joyful and happy approach to life. It promotes an ability to entertain. Creativity is enhanced. It colours the Name Number with the art of mixing well; the ability to socialize. Gregariousness is helped.

4: Intensifies a practical and orthodox attitude to living. The ability to cope with detailed work and the patience to finish whatever is started. The Name Number is coloured with a single-minded attitude to work, a degree of workaholism.

5: Intensifies the need for freedom and change. It adds versatility, an awareness of sexual needs and the ability to adapt to quickly changing circumstances. It colours the Name Number with communicative ability and motivation of others.

6: Intensifies a feeling of responsibility and need for justice. It aids creative and vocal work. Encourages over-eating. The ability to teach is enhanced. The Name Number is coloured with a sense of harmony and balance.

7: Intensifies a need for solitude. Use of analysis and intuition is encouraged. Personal experience is needed – making one's own mistakes. Being taught by others is disliked. Metaphysical interests are likely. It colours the Name Number with mystery.

8: Intensifies the development of a businesslike and efficient attitude. Dependability and organization are enhanced. Financial acumen is strong. Physical interests, sport and so on, can be encouraged. It colours the Name Number with power and the need for success.

9: Intensifies the development of a compassionate and tolerant attitude. There is a dramatic intensity and emotional magnetism attached to this number. Humanitarian values are enhanced. A love of travel, romance and the holding of idealistic views are all strengthened. A broad-minded outlook colours the Name Number.

THE MISSING NUMBERS

Any number, from 1 to 9, that does not appear in your name represents a missing quality; if this number does not appear elsewhere, you will have to consciously develop it.

Numerologists who believe the name on the birth certificate is all-important regard a missing number as having karmic implications. The number represents a lesson to be learnt in this life; something that was ignored or misused in a previous incarnation. The missing number becomes a number of Karma.

Whether you believe this or not, a number missing from the name you use represents something that is lacking. If the number is not elsewhere (the birth numbers, Vowel, Consonant, Name or First Name) you will have to develop it.

The numbers 1 and 9 will be present on all Birthcharts for babies born up to 31.12.1999; the number 2 on all Birthcharts from 1.1.2000.

The following name, a fairly common one, has the numbers 3 and 7 missing. If found nowhere else, the person using this name would need to work harder than most to develop these qualities.

```
        6               9
    J O H N     S M I T H
    1   8 5     1 4   2 8
```

MEANING OF THE MISSING NUMBERS

1: Originality is missing. The person needs to develop initiative, self-assertion, the will-to-win, self-confidence, the ability to lead, ambition, a strong will-power and determination.

2: Sensitivity is missing. The person needs to develop the ability to cooperate with others, to be able to work in a team, to follow directions, show friendliness, kindness and awareness of the feelings of others.

3: Creativity is missing. The person needs to develop a less serious outlook, a joy for living, behave gregariously, have a sense of humour, be optimistic, be sociable and use the imagination.

4: Patience is missing. The person needs to develop practicality, stability, tenacity, attention to detail, the ability to work long and hard, a constructive outlook, a degree of self-discipline.

5: Versatility is missing. The person needs to develop adaptability, a willingness to try anything new, not be afraid of progress, learn how to communicate, to show enthusiasm, to motivate others, to be adventurous.

6: Responsibility is missing. The person needs to develop a well-balanced outlook, an appreciation of beauty and the arts, creativeness, a sense of honour, to be able to harmonize divergent aspects of the life, to learn how to teach.

7: Self-examination is missing. The person needs to develop spiritual awareness, to be unafraid of solitude, to gain self-reliance, to use intuition and analysis, to learn by experience, to develop inner strength.

8: Financial acumen is missing. The person needs to develop efficiency, dependability, the ability to organize, to set realistic goals, to help others in need, to develop physical stamina, to be independent, and to be able to use power wisely.

9: Generosity is missing. The person needs to develop high ideals, humanitarian instincts, compassion, to be broad-minded and tolerant, use creativity, be unafraid of the romantic and the dramatic, to learn how to love without seeking reward.

THE NAMECHART

The numbers of your name can be used in the same way as your birth numbers by placing them on a chart: the Namechart. This shows (just as the Birthchart) the pattern of strengths and weaknesses – this time from your name.

The numbers are placed in the same positions as on the Birthchart (see Chapter 3, p.20). You will find it interesting to compare both charts. If your Birthchart is weak, with many missing numbers (this will be especially so after 2000 AD, showing the need for those born at the start of a new millennium to consciously develop and grow), a good Namechart will provide you with additional strength. The imbalance caused by missing numbers on the Birthchart is somewhat eliminated when the numbers appear on the Namechart.

If your Birthchart is strong, with many numbers and Lines, your Namechart may provide too much strength if it duplicates the Birthchart numbers. It will not then be considered 'balanced', but it can create a charismatic or strong type of person.

It is always better if any missing Birthchart numbers are present on the Namechart. It makes life easier.

Tennessee

Zsa Zsa

2	5 5 5 5 5 5	
1 1		

		8 8
1 1 1 1		

Chart 6: Namecharts for Tennessee and Zsa Zsa

Place the numbers contained within your first name on the Namechart first. This is your most important individual name, so its effect is the most striking. In Chart 6, we see the first names of the writer, Tennessee Williams, and the actress, Zsa Zsa Gabor. Tennessee and Zsa Zsa as first names dramatically intensify the Namechart.

These names would encourage their possessors to display distinctive attributes. They would not guarantee fame to anyone else, but the effect felt from the name would be similar.

The vibrations from all those 5s in Tennessee (six in a nine-letter name) would assist communication, sexuality – all five senses enhanced; the name Zsa Zsa has strong concentration on the number 1 (four in a six-letter name), encouraging leadership and originality, backed by the material power of the number 8. A possibly ambitious combination. Obviously, the person's other numerological combinations have to be considered.

After analysing your first name, place your last or other names on the chart. Compare your complete Namechart with your Birthchart. Does it over-strengthen certain numbers? Does it replicate a Line? This increases the possibility of your name creating too much strength that will be difficult to handle.

Chart 7 shows the Birthchart and Namechart of the playwright, Eugene O'Neill: His Namechart and Birthchart compliment each other; combined, he had only the 2 and 4 as missing numbers. This is a powerful name that balances well the numbers of birth.

Birthchart: 10.16.1888   Name chart Eugene O'Neill

	6	
		8 8 8
1 1 1		

3 3 3	6	9
	5 5 5 5 5 5	
		7

Chart 7: Eugene O'Neill's Birthchart and Namechart

Always remember, the name is an outside influence and will never create the strength represented by your birth date and Life Path.

THE SUBMERGED CHARACTERISTIC

The Submerged Characteristic is a less important number. It is hidden most of the time. Sometimes called the Habit, or the Habit Challenge, you will be aware of this hidden strength but will use it only occasionally. It is mainly used when problems cannot easily be solved.

The Submerged Characteristic is found by adding together the number of letters you have in your complete name. Not the value of the letters but *how many* you have. Fadic addition, as always, is used.

George Bush has ten letters in his name – 10, 1+0 = 1 – his Submerged Characteristic is 1; Golda Meir had nine letters, her Submerged Characteristic was 9.

MEANING OF THE SUBMERGED CHARACTERISTIC

1: An original approach will be found. This will take others by surprise. A determination to take the initiative brings speedy results.

2: The ability to let others lead; to follow or obey orders when necessary. Collaboration can be successful. Diplomatic skills are in evidence.

3: Imagination and creativity used when problems seem insoluble. There will be an artistic approach. Difficulties not always taken seriously.

4: Realistic objectives will be approached logically. Detailed analysis will be employed. A practical and orthodox solution will be preferred. Uninvolved emotionally.

5: The ability to accept change. A new, untried solution can succeed. Risks will be taken. Quickness and versatility surfaces.

6: Responsible decisions that take account of all involved will be employed. The effect on family life will be considered. A sympathetic approach.

7: Solutions are found within oneself. There is a disinclination to take advice. The person will not want to act until conditions are perfect. Meditative.

8: Efficiency can be used in a ruthless manner. Definite results and goals will be the aim of any problem solving. Slow and steady works best.

9: A broad-minded view will be taken. Generosity extended towards others. Idealistic in approach. If opposed, reactions can be unexpected and dramatic.

10 · THE TEMPERAMENT AND CHOOSING A NAME

> No, Groucho is not my real name. I'm breaking it in for a friend.
>
> Groucho Marx

The letters in your name affect the way you carry out your plans. Two people may have the same Name Number – but the letters behind it show how they prefer to express themselves: either mentally, physically, emotionally or intuitively. To find this we use the Temperament Chart. Some numerologists prefer the term: Planes of Expression.

We express ourselves in four different ways: some people think things out, calculate the odds, weigh everything up in their minds before reacting; others do everything by instinct; while some listen to their heart or their emotions; others prefer an active or practical approach. The Temperament Chart shows how your name influences *your* response. Chart 8 (overleaf) shows where each letter of the alphabet is placed.

The Mental Letters indicate a thinking approach. Decisions are made coolly and calmly. Instinctive or emotional judgements will not be rushed into. A majority of letters here does not, unfortunately, make you a genius – but you will always think things out before acting.

	Mental	Physical	Emotional	Intuitive
Starters	A	E	I O R Z	K
Improvers	H J N P	W	B S T X	F Q U Y
Finishers	G L	D M		C V

Chart 8: The Temperament Chart

The Physical Letters show a need for taking action rather than sitting around thinking. A majority of letters here indicates promotion of energy, keeping busy. Emotions and intuition take second place. The person needs to act rather than consider.

The Emotional Letters show the heart and dreams are always considered. A majority of letters here indicates decisions based on desire. Artistic awareness is present.

The Intuitive Letters show instinct is always relied on. There is a degree of psychic awareness. Names containing a majority of intuitive letters help develop a knowledge of the spirit. There is often a dreamlike quality about this person. Their approach to life will not appear practical.

The section that contains most of your letters reveals your principal way of expressing yourself or taking decisions. If this section has considerably more letters than any other, this part of your temperament will be notably strong. If there is little to choose between all four sections, then your name and temperament are well-balanced.

From the Temperament, you can see which type of career your name *ideally* helps. Most letters in the Mental section assist cerebral or sedentary work. The Physical section promotes physical or practical work. The Emotional helps artistic or creative careers: the theatre, fashion or creative hobbies. The Intuitive Letters assist unorthodox types of employment or spiritual or religious careers.

The letters are also divided into three sections (see Chapter 8, p.69): Starters, Improvers and Finishers. Where you have the most letters shows how your name helps you begin, continue or finish projects.

Place *all* your letters in their respective positions on the chart. Add together the amount of letters contained separately in each section. Use fadic addition. As an example, here (in Chart 9) is the name of the French writer, Jean-Paul Sartre:

	Mental	Physical	Emotional	Intuitive	
Starters	A A A	E E	R R		7
Improvers	J N P		S T	U	6
Finishers	L				1
	7	2	4	1	

Chart 9: Jean-Paul Satre's Temperament Chart

Notice the dominance of the number 7 (the deep thinker) in both the Mental and Starter sections (p.69). The majority of his letters are in the Mental section. Here is someone who will have a clear intellectual view about what he is doing in life. When final decisions are necessary, he will follow his mind rather than his heart. The 7 here shows a concern with the inner meaning of life. His emotional feelings will be dealt with in a practical way – here he has a 4. Physically he has a 2 and should be able to cooperate in ordinary everyday affairs; intuition comes in an inspired way or quick as a flash – the number 1.

He is able to initiate projects and continue with them once

started. Although he can finish what he begins, the single 1 in the Finisher section (p.70) indicates difficulties at times.

THE TEMPERAMENT NUMBERS

NUMBER 1

Mental: An original thinker. The ability to conceive new and exciting ways of doing things. Can dominate discussions sometimes. May show impatience.

Physical: Can show leadership qualities. There is a need to keep busy. Active, with a sense of humour. Can be brusque.

Emotional: Prefers to be the dominant partner in a relationship. Is optimistic and original. There may be a dislike of psychoanalysis.

Intuitive: New and original ideas appear as if from nowhere. Good creative instincts which can be used with enthusiasm.

NUMBER 2

Mental: Enjoys collecting knowledge and is good at detailed work. Finds it easy to collaborate or work with others. Can see both sides of the question.

Physical: Can easily work as part of a team. Is able to improve things that others have started. May have artistic hobbies or interests. Can be over-polite.

Emotional: Has a need for companionship. Feels lost without somebody to share with. Extremely sensitive to the needs of others. Over-sensitive at times.

Intuitive: Uses intuition easily. Is sensitive to atmosphere. This number here helps psychic qualities unfold. Spiritually aware. May hesitate to act.

NUMBER 3

Mental: Brings creativity to any mental problem. Life is not always taken seriously. A sense of the absurd. Needs constant stimulation.

Physical: Self-expressive and artistic. Often a popular person.

Joie de vivre. Easily bored. Restlessness and carelessness can be shown. Full of fun.

Emotional: Can easily express desires, dreams and love. Likes receiving affection and wants it to be shown. Witty, with creative talents. Moves on when bored.

Intuitive: Instinct and intuition are used creatively. Is imaginative and artistic in feelings. There can be an attraction towards ritual.

NUMBER 4

Mental: Uses logic to approach any mental problem. Is practical and orthodox in ideas. Distrusts anything too original. Makes constructive and workable plans.

Physical: Can work hard and feels uneasy with nothing to do. May have a talent for using the hands in some way.

Emotional: Practical matters are always considered. Is serious in emotions. Can be loyal. There may be a feeling of restriction.

Intuitive: Either distrusts the inner voice, or feels more comfortable following a logical, practical path. May ignore intuition. Orthodox in religion or agnostic.

NUMBER 5

Mental: A quick and versatile mind. No restrictions on interests. Bright conversationalist. May change interests suddenly. Attracted to the new.

Physical: Works well with others. Active and athletic with a competitive instinct. Adapts well to change and copes extremely well in a crisis.

Emotional: Seeks freedom and dislikes being tied down. Changes interests and affections easier than most. Popular, adventurous and exciting.

Intuitive: Attuned to the reactions of others. Good instincts but often distrusts them and may need proof before acting.

NUMBER 6

Mental: Brings responsibility to the thinking process. Can be a creative problem-solver. Understands the difficulties of others.

Physical: Balances work and home life in equal proportion and needs both. Works well with or for others. Needs to have beauty around. Can show creativity.

Emotional: Artistic interests are important but will sacrifice much for a stable domestic background. Can accept responsibility easily.

Intuitive: Must trust instinct more than trusting other people. Keeps a good balance between intuition and fact. Inclined to meddle.

NUMBER 7

Mental: Needs solitude to make decisions. Good analytical ability. Sees a lot but keeps silent. Dislikes interference in decisionmaking.

Physical: Active, but prefers working alone to being part of a team. Dislikes a noisy or crowded environment. Puzzling to others.

Emotional: Capable of deep emotional commitment but dislikes others knowing this. A need to achieve perfection in everything.

Intuitive: A strong inner voice that needs to be acted on; sometimes it is ignored. Good evaluation of others' needs. Spiritually strong.

NUMBER 8

Mental: Powerful and efficient business sense. A need to succeed. Has to beware of materialistic greed. Strong and tough debater.

Physical: Athletic ability enhanced. Becomes a prominent figure in any team-work. Sets targets to aim at. Realistic and dependable.

Emotional: Career interests usually put first. Will try to dominate in relationships. Staunch ally in a crisis or in a time of need.

Intuitive: Can use intuition to help others less fortunate. Is able to mix spirituality with materialism to good effect.

NUMBER 9

Mental: Has a wide vision of what is needed to be done. Dislikes dealing with details. Idealistic. Humanitarian values kept in mind.

Physical: Dramatic and artistic expression usually preferred. Brings an inspired approach to mundane matters. Shows compassion to others.

Emotional: Romantic and deep feelings are affected by this number. Melodramatic at times – up one minute, down the next. Can be too trusting.

Intuitive: Attuned to a higher consciousness. Inspired dreams may sometimes create impracticality. Strong spiritual beliefs.

ZERO ON THE TEMPERAMENT CHART

Mental: A dislike of taking decisions (or making them) based on fact. Lack of confidence in using logical thought. Difficulty studying.

Physical: Physical stamina and endurance is not marked. There can be difficulty in dealing with life in a practical manner. May need motivating.

Emotional: Emotional feeling is repressed or there is a difficulty in expressing it. Life seems dull at times. Understands others with difficulty.

Intuitive: A disinclination to follow hunches or instincts. Lack of interest in the spiritual world or metaphysical topics. Has difficulty coping with the abstract.

LOOKING FOR HARMONY IN YOUR NUMBERS

You can now compare the numbers of your birth date and name together. It is interesting to see how they interact.

Your two most important numbers are your Life Path and Name Number. As stated earlier, if they are the same, you have the perfect combination. The next best combination is if they are both odd or both even – with this there is still harmony. If one is odd and the other even there is conflict; although life is not so smooth it provides opportunities to grow stronger as you surmount any problems.

A quick and easy way to see the general harmony of your life is to compare your Life Path, Name and Power (remembering the Power Number is found by adding the Life Path and Name Numbers together). For example:

Life Path 4   Name 4   Power 8   =   a perfect combination
Life Path 2   Name 6   Power 8   =   a harmonious combination.
Life Path 3   Name 4   Power 7   =   a conflicting combination

More detail is acquired by comparing all your *main* numbers. Your Life Path is the key. If other numbers do not conflict with your Life Path success comes easier; difficult future events are easier to cope with. If the Name Number conflicts, but the other numbers are harmonious, there may still be dissatisfaction felt in what is being achieved. Achievement refers to not only material success but spiritual and emotional as well.

To assess your main characteristics, use only the following numbers: Life Path (LP); Birthday (B); Goal (G); Name Number (N); Vowel Number (V); Consonant Number (C); First Name (FN); First Letter (FL); First Vowel (FV); Power (P); and your Intensity Number (I) – but only if your Intensity is represented by a single number, not two or three.

Write the numbers 1 to 9 in a line and place your main numbers underneath. Use initials for their names. Here are the numbers of the former British Prime Minister, Margaret Thatcher. She was born on 13 October 1925.

1	2	3	4	5	6	7	8	9
FV1	FN2		LP4	G5			P8	C9
			B4					
			N4					
			V4					
			FL4					

There is no single Intensity Number. This is an excellent chart. Observe the strong support for her 4 Life Path. Accepting the opportunities for hard work and self-discipline that the 4 Life Path brings would be no problem for a person with these supporting numbers.

It is fatuous to believe a harmonious arrangement of numbers brings untold worldly success – but it does help expression of the person's full potential. The life *is* easier. The person appears to be in the right place at the right time.

CHOOSING A NAME

Using numerology, you can select the 'right' name for a child; but do not choose a name simply because of its numbers. It must be a name that is liked and that you would want to bestow regardless of what it adds up to.

The date of birth has to be known – in other words, the child must be born. This should not stop you preparing a list of suitable names before the birth.

For a suitable name the rules are simple: the Name Number (this is first and last names together) should be the same number as the Life Path, or at least harmonious (both odd or both even).

The First Name Number should not be the same as the Birthday (even if Birthday and Life Path are the same).

It should be the name you intend to use. If you decide on Joanna, then address the child as Jo, the numbers will not be the same. It is the name that is used on a daily basis that is important – the name the child thinks of as his or her own.

You should also compare all the child's numbers and take note of the pattern on the Namechart.

There is nothing to stop you giving your child any number of names to go on the birth certificate. It is the name that is used day after day that is important. These are the vibrations that have the ultimate effect. As the Bible states: 'A good name is rather to be had than great riches.'

If, in later years, your child chooses another name, it should not be taken as a rejection of you or your values. He or she has a right to choose something else. Just as you do.

CHANGING A NAME

It is important to treat this seriously, to take your time over it, and not decide to change your name on a whim – this is because it *does* work. A name change changes your life in some way. If the new name greatly improves the look of the numbers on a chart, a marked new philosophical outlook will emerge and fortunate opportunities appear.

This is why a name change is common when people commit themselves to a spiritual or religious path – because it works. And why there is often distrust or ridicule aimed at a person who has changed a name. This reflects the subconscious fear that the person is hiding a part of themselves – in other words, the new name reflects a different personality. The change works. A different image is projected. Regimented societies or class-conscious cultures are usually suspicious of name changing. A wish to control the name is a wish to control the individual.

Changing the name is, however fanciful it sounds, a form of magic. It is the conscious act of choosing a different personal symbol. You are changing your power.

Any change will not happen overnight. It will usually take years before the full effect is noted, but it starts from day one. There is a saying: 'If you want to change the world, start with yourself.'

A change can mean an alteration in the spelling, or a slight rearrangement of the letters. This is far easier to put into practice than taking a completely different name. Always consider this option first. But you are living your life, and no-one has any right to tell you what name you should be called. It is your name. If you prefer to answer to a different sound – you have that right.

A period of confusion usually follows any sort of name alteration. Adjustments in the life have to be made. Some people find difficulty coping with this period and revert to the former name. There is nothing wrong in doing this.

The rules for changing a name are the same as choosing a name for a child: the Life Path and Name Number should match (or be harmonious); the First Name should not match the Birthday; and all the important numbers should be considered.

As a judge said to the newly-named film magnate, Samuel Goldwyn (of Metro-Goldwyn-Mayer fame, after changing his name from Goldfish), 'A self-made man may prefer a self-made name.'

11 · THE CYCLE AND YEAR NUMBERS

> When one has much to put into them, a day has a hundred
> pockets.
>
> Friedrich Nietzsche

The opportunities that occur in your life appear in cycles.
Numerology can show this but it does not make predictions; it
does not tell your fortune. What happens tomorrow is affected
by what you do today. But it can show the *probable* events
and opportunities you will encounter. What happens when
you encounter them is up to you. So there *is* a right time and
a right place and this can be calculated; but it is *your* actions
that will take advantage of any opportunities.

Your full birth date is the foundation the cycles in your
life have developed from. You have many different cycles all
occurring at the same time. This chapter and the following one
will show how to find the most important. It is the expertise
you use to analyse the combined effect of these numbers that
determines how effective your forecasting is.

THE THREE CYCLES OF LIFE

Your life is divided into three stages or cycles. The first is
represented by the fadic number of your month of birth; the

second, by the fadic number of your day of birth; the third by the number of your birth year after using fadic addition.

Dates in America are written with the month first; in Britain, with the birth day first. In this chapter, the American system will be used; this is the conventional way to calculate cycles in numerology. Wherever you were born, for the following calculations always use this order: Birth Month, Birth Day, Birth Year.

The following birth date belongs to the former Soviet President, Nikita Khrushchev: 4.17.1894. After fadic addition, his date looks like this: 4.8.4. His First Cycle (his month number) would be under the vibration of 4; his Second (his day number) under 8; his Third (his year number) under 4.

Your First Cycle begins when you are born. To find when your Second Cycle starts, you deduct your Life Path Number from the number 36 (this number, 36, which is 9 multiplied by 4, has a powerful occult symbolism attached to it). Your Second Cycle lasts 27 years (9 multiplied by 3) and is followed by your Third Cycle, which lasts until death or until Samuel Butler's description of this transition happens: '. . . a larger kind of going abroad'.

Each cycle shows the general trend behind a part of your life.

Life Path 1: Second Cycle begins at 35, Third Cycle at 62
Life Path 2: Second Cycle begins at 34, Third Cycle at 61
Life Path 3: Second Cycle begins at 33, Third Cycle at 60
Life Path 4: Second Cycle begins at 32, Third Cycle at 59
Life Path 5: Second Cycle begins at 31, Third Cycle at 58
Life Path 6: Second Cycle begins at 30, Third Cycle at 57
Life Path 7: Second Cycle begins at 29, Third Cycle at 56
Life Path 8: Second Cycle begins at 28, Third Cycle at 55
Life Path 9: Second Cycle begins at 27, Third Cycle at 54

CYCLE NUMBERS

Cycle 1: A need to stand on one's own feet. Events instil a degree of independence. The person considers his or her own needs. Impatience is felt at times. New opportunities often occur. Leadership will be conferred at some time –

even if unwanted. The person needs to be self-reliant, to be decisive.

Cycle 2: Opportunities to mix with groups, to work in large organizations or become attached to teams. The person is sensitive to the opinions of others. There are many friends and public recognition can occur, although often unsought. There is a need for companionship. Events develop slowly. The person may have to follow the direction of others.

Cycle 3: A pleasant cycle in which creative work can prosper, although there is a likelihood opportunities may be squandered in order to have a good time. The social scene dominates the life. An enjoyment of entertaining or mixing with others is present. The person appears 'lucky'. Restlessness and boredom often occur. A need for excitement.

Cycle 4: Practical matters need to be tackled. There is a good deal of hard work. The person feels restricted at times. The opportunity occurs to lay steady foundations for progress at work or at home. The person needs to relax or play more. Life is taken seriously. Life is busy. A need to guard against getting into a rut.

Cycle 5: Circumstances change frequently. Surprising adventures occur – often unlooked-for. There is difficulty staying in one career. Interests can change. The person will display adaptability. Communicating with others is important. Travel and opportunities to try 'anything new' are available. Competitive situations dominate.

Cycle 6: There are many creative opportunities during this cycle but the attention may be focused on the home. The domestic environment is important. Responsibility is taken on. The person is often asked for advice. A need for love in the life. Searching for 'balance' at all times. The domestic environment is either harmonious or disruptive.

Cycle 7: There is a lot of inner searching or psychoanalysing oneself in this cycle. The person feels confused in noisy or bustling environments. There is a need for solitude. Much personal growth can take place. It is difficult to force the pace of material progress. Opportunities occur suddenly. Action is quickly taken after much thought. The person can reject advice and create difficulties.

Cycle 8: Slow and steady progress is made towards personal goals – but the work needs to be done. This is a good financial cycle, but only if it is earned. A tendency to be over-ambitious at times. Independence is important, goals will be set. There is a karmic feel to this cycle – good or bad – the person gets what is deserved. Effort is needed.

Cycle 9: Anything is possible under this number. It is good for creative matters, especially the serious arts. Often there is difficulty in starting new projects; sometimes unaccountable endings. This is an emotional cycle and restraint is needed sometimes. Practical matters need more attention. Travel and a wide circle of friends or contacts are indicated.

THE CHALLENGE

Behind each individual cycle is a Challenge: this shows inhibitions or self-imposed restrictions that must be conquered for attaining fulfilment.

The First Challenge operates during the First Cycle; the Second Challenge is in force during the Second Cycle; the Third Challenge is the most important; it operates during the Third Cycle but its restrictions are felt throughout the life. As we age, the challenges have less power. They have usually been acknowledged and conquered.

The First Challenge is found by subtracting your fadic Month Number from your Birthday Number (or the smaller from the larger); the Second Challenge by subtracting your Birthday from your fadic Year of Birth Number; the Third Challenge by subtracting your First Challenge Number from your Second Challenge Number.

This birth date, 11.22.1943, belongs to the tennis player, Billie Jean King. After fadic addition her birth date looks like this: 2.4.8. Her First Challenge is 2 (4−2 = 2); her Second Challenge is 4 (8−4 = 4); her Third Challenge is 2 (4−2 = 2).

THE CHALLENGE NUMBERS

Zero Challenge: There is no individual Challenge. This does not mean there is no individual negative quality to overcome – only that it will constantly change.

1 Challenge: There is reluctance to take a leadership role, to take the initiative. There is a fear of independence.

2 Challenge: There is a lack of awareness of the needs of others. A disinclination to cooperate. A lack of sensitivity.

3 Challenge: There is a reluctance to enjoy life or be frivolous. Creativity may be squandered. A difficulty in self-expression.

4 Challenge: There is a dislike of looking at life realistically or in a practical way. There is difficulty in getting out of a rut.

5 Challenge: There is a fear of the new, of taking a risk. There will be disinterest in communicating with others.

6 Challenge: There is the possibility of disruption in domestic concerns unless a balance is attained. A dislike of responsibility.

7 Challenge: There is a dislike of solitude. A fear of examining one's own motives. A lack of faith.

8 Challenge: There is a reluctance to accept personal power. The life feels disjointed. There is greed.

THE TURNING POINTS

There are four Turning Points in your life. Significant events occur at these times. Sometimes they will not be recognized as such until later. During these Turning Points you have a heightened inner energy. This helps you meet your opportunities in a positive manner.

The First Point is found by deducting your Life Path Number from the number 36 (it is the same age as the beginning of your Second Cycle). Your next three Turning Points occur every nine years.

The Turning Points occur at the following ages:

Life Path 1: at ages 35, 44, 53 and 62
Life Path 2: at ages 34, 43, 52 and 61
Life Path 3: at ages 33, 42, 51 and 60
Life Path 4: at ages 32, 41, 50 and 59
Life Path 5: at ages 31, 40, 49 and 58
Life Path 6: at ages 30, 39, 48 and 57
Life Path 7: at ages 29, 38, 47 and 56
Life Path 8: at ages 28, 37, 46 and 55
Life Path 9: at ages 27, 36, 45 and 54

The Turning Point lasts for one year but its effects can be experienced over a longer period. It can be felt up to one year before it begins and the effects can last for three to four years, although the full potent effect will be felt during its first year of transit. To find the number vibration for each individual Turning Point:

First Turning Point: add your Birth Month and Birthday together fadically.
Second Turning Point: add your Birthday and Birth Year together fadically.
Third Turning Point: add the numbers of your First and Second Points together fadically.
Fourth Turning Point: add your Birth Month and Birth Year together fadically.

For example: the numbers of the Turning Points in the life of the actor Marlon Brando, who was born 4.3.1924 (4.3.7), are: 7 for his First (4+3 = 7); his Second was 1 (3+7 = 10, 1+0 = 1); his Third was 8 (7+1 = 8); and his Fourth was 2 (4+7 = 11, 1+1 = 2).

TURNING POINT NUMBERS

Turning Point 1: A new direction in life appears. There is the opportunity to gain independence. The person is concerned with personal needs.

Turning Point 2: A partnership can begin. There is a need to mix with people. Psychic ability is enhanced and the person is aware of the needs of others.

Turning Point 3: Pleasure and social events dominate. Travel is likely. The mental and creative powers are used fully.

Turning Point 4: There is much work but it is coped with easily. An opportunity to lay strong foundations for the rest of the life occurs.

Turning Point 5: Something new and completely unexpected appears in the life. A need for freedom is felt. A progressive opportunity should be grasped.

Turning Point 6: Creative matters come to the fore. A lot of interest is centred on the home. Responsibilities are easily handled. Love, marriage or divorce is possible.

Turning Point 7: Individuality is strengthened and personal motivation is better understood. Opportunities occur out of the blue. A mysterious time that is understood better afterwards.

Turning Point 8: Material success can be attained. Opportunities to gain independence can be earned. A good time financially.

Turning Point 9: An established part of the life can end. There is a great change, often confusion, often travel. The person is highly emotional but emerges stronger and more compassionate after it is over.

UNIVERSAL YEAR, MONTH AND DAY

The calendar date shows the vibrations for each particular day. How you are affected depends on the combined effect of your other numbers.

The Universal Year Number is the number of each year after using fadic addition. The numbers behind the fadic number are important but are not usually considered in conventional numerology. The Universal Year Number for 1999 is 1 (1+9+9+9 = 28, 2+8 = 10, 1+0 = 1); the Universal Year Number for 2000 is 2 (2+0+0+0 = 2).

To find the Universal Month you add the calendar number of the month in question to the Universal Year Number: December 1999 is 4 (1+2+1 = 4).

The Universal Day is (either the calendar day added to the Universal Month or) the fadic total of the full date: 31 December 1999 is 8 (3+1+1+2+1+9+9+9 = 35, 3+5 = 8). It is interesting to see the last day of the present millennium is 8, which has been called in the past the 'number of karma' (we receive what we deserve), and the first Universal Day of the year 2000 is a 4 (an opportunity to lay firm foundations for the future).

For matters, projects, interests or events that concern you and for which you need the cooperation of others – or anything that you cannot put into operation without outside help – you will need to consider the Universal Day. Using the day when the universal vibrations will help you is wise. The Universal Day that matches your Life Path Number is considered 'lucky' for you.

The effects of the Universal vibrations (Years, Months and Days) are listed together here:

1 *Vibration*: New starts, opportunities, independence, starting anew.
2 *Vibration*: A quiet time, consolidating, cooperating, teamwork.
3 *Vibration*: Entertainment, self-expression, sociability, travel.
4 *Vibration*: Laying plans, practicality, organization, working-hard.
5 *Vibration*: Exciting changes, communication, travel, sexual attraction.
6 *Vibration*: Home activities, creativity, responsibilities, marriage.
7 *Vibration*: Inner-searching, study, rest, unexpected surprises.
8 *Vibration*: Material success or failure, independence, goals achieved.
9 *Vibration*: Humanitarian matters, idealism, endings, high drama.

PERSONAL YEAR, MONTH AND DAY

The way you react to the Universal vibrations around you is influenced by the numbers of your Personal Year, Month and Day.

Your Personal Year starts on the 1st January each year (although you will feel its vibrations from October onward of the preceding year; it will continue to operate, weakening, into the following year until the start of a 1 Personal Month). To find its number, add your Birthday and Month Numbers together (this is, as you will have realized, your Goal Number) to the year in question. For example: if your Birthday and Month are 5 and 5, and you wanted to find out what opportunities 1999 would bring – you would add $5+5+1+9+9+9 = 38$, $3+8 = 11$, $1+1 = 2$. 1999 would be a 2 Personal Year for you.

To find your Personal Month Number, add the calendar number of the month to your Personal Year Number. To find December for the above 2 Personal Year, you would add 12 and 2, $1+2+2 = 5$. December in 1999 would be a 5 Personal Month.

To find your Personal Day Number, add the number of the day to your Personal Month. 31st December in the above example would be $3+1+5 = 9$. A 9 Personal Day.

For someone with a 5 Birthday and 5 Birth Month Number, the date 12.31.1999 would work out as a 2 Personal Year, 5 Personal Month and a 9 Personal Day. All three numbers would be operating on a personal level for that person on that day. The Universal vibrations should not, of course, be forgotten.

Dramatic words are often used by numerologists to describe the effect of the numbers. Obviously, everyday life is not so colourful; most of the time life is repetitive or mundane. Fanciful language is used to give a flavour of what is ultimately possible, as here.

PERSONAL VIBRATIONS

Personal 1 Vibration: A time to begin life anew. The ability to start afresh. New directions and opportunities are offered and should be accepted. Independence is easier to gain than usual. A self-confident phase. An energizing time.

Personal 2 Vibration: A peaceful and calm period after the 1. There is time to think and consolidate plans. Friendships and partnerships prosper. It is easier than usual to cooperate with others. Sensitivity is enhanced. Affection and love are felt.

Personal 3 Vibration: A happy, joyous period. Imaginative affairs and creative use of the mind prosper. Travel is likely. There are many opportunities to join gatherings, to mingle and socialize. An optimistic period. There is an element of good luck.

Personal 4 Vibration: Patience and organization pay off. A realistic attitude prevails. A practical period when the opportunity to make plans and build stronger foundations for what has already been established prevails. A stable time.

Personal 5 Vibration: New opportunities occur. Change is in the air. Freedom is sought. New people or interests come into the life. Under this number adaptability is stronger than usual. There are many sensual attractions. A second chance (after 1) to start afresh.

Personal 6 Vibration: Domestic matters occupy a lot of time. The best number for love or marriage. Responsibilities are taken on more willingly than usual. Obligations and duties are attended to. Creative endeavours are favoured.

Personal 7 Vibration: Important insight into one's own motives occurs. Rest and reflection are needed. There is a stronger need than usual to spend time alone. Frustration can be experienced materially and then, when least expected, surprising victories occur.

Personal 8 Vibration: Success and material achievement can be gained, but only if they have been worked for. A good business vibration. Independence is won. There is a need to push hard for things under this number. A balance between the material and spiritual brings success.

Personal 9 Vibration: Unlooked-for endings occur – but only what is no longer needed. The dross is shifted from the life. Opportunities to show compassion and understanding appear. An emotional and dramatic time. Idealistic and romantic.

Travel can feature. A number of fulfilment but not especially good for new starts – make plans to begin again in 1.

In practice you may find the Personal Year and Personal Month an accurate guide to your *opportunities* for the month and year; the Universal Day reliable for *instigating* action on a daily basis; the Personal Day instructive for *inner* needs.

12 · THE TRANSIT AND EVENT NUMBERS

There's a divinity that shapes our ends, rough-hew them how we will.

William Shakespeare

Forecasts can be made relating to events in your life by using your full birth name – this is the name *as written* on your birth certificate. This appears a bizarre practice or belief but can be uncannily accurate. There are many things in life we cannot explain or scientifically prove – from intuition to religious belief – and it is necessary sometimes to keep an open mind; you will be able to examine your past life with this technique and prove to yourself if it works or not.

The full name on your birth certificate is needed. It is what you started out with even if it is no longer, or has never been, used. The correct wording on the birth certificate means any misspellings or extraneous words that occur. Each letter in your name affects your life for a particular year or years. The letters (as used in this way) are called the Letters of Transit.

Write down your full name (exactly as written on the birth certificate) with the number values of the letters on top. As an example, we will use the name Ann Rose Smith:

```
1 5 5        9 6 1 5      1 4 9 2 8
A N N        R O S E      S M I T H
```

Each letter transits your life for the same number of years as its value (A being 1 would be activated for one year; N being 5 would be activated for 5 years). After the transits of all the letters in a name you return to the first letter to repeat the process. Each individual name is analysed separately: Ann, Rose and Smith are treated individually and not together as Ann Rose Smith.

The transits begin on the day you are born. Place 0 under each first letter. Your second letter starts after the required number of years of your first letter has ended. In our example, A being 1 transits for the first twelve months of life (1 year) and N starts at the first birthday.

```
1   5   5      9   6   1   5      1   4   9   2   8
A   N   N      R   O   S   E      S   M   I   T   H
0   1   6      0   9   15  16     0   1   5   14  16
11  12  17     21  30  36  37     24  25  29  38  40
22  23  28     42  51  57  58     48  49  53  62  64
33  34  39     63  72  78  79     72  73  77  86  88
```

Looking at Ann Rose Smith (with three names she will always have three letters in transit at any one time), we see the A of Ann affected her first year; the R of Rose influenced her first nine years; and the S of Smith was in operation for her first year of life (or until she had the S again at twenty-four years of age).

If we wanted to find the likely events she would encounter aged eighteen, we would refer to her name and see that N, E and H were then in transit.

Care should be taken calculating the transits. It is simple to do but mistakes are common. A single error will disrupt your forecasting.

It is possible to set up a chart for a new name if you know the exact year the name was taken. But the complete birth name will always still apply. The name you are *known* by, if it is harmonious with your Life Path, will ease difficult transits; a conflicting name does not help. The Letters of Transit operate from birthday to birthday, not from the 1st of January as the Personal Year does.

Two or more of the same letters (for instance: two As) transiting at the same time may create a strong but difficult period.

THE LETTERS OF TRANSIT

A (1 year): Change, new starts, beginnings. A change of direction in the career, or a change of home. Creative projects begun.
AA: Over-active. May miss opportunities.

B (2 years): A slower pace is indicated. Partnerships or love affairs favoured. Excessive nervousness possible and health needs watching.
BB: An over-emotional period.

C (3 years): Creativity enhanced. Social events are highlighted. Domestic disharmony is possible. An enjoyable time but restless.
CC: Play too hard. Extremely restless.

D (4 years): Opportunities to organize and take responsibility for one's own life. Practical, hard-working period. Rest is needed.
DD: Workaholism. Life seems limited.

E (5 years): Freedom is sought. Exciting changes and meeting of new people. Opportunity for travel and new love affairs. Eccentric period.
EE: Changing of ideas and interests too often.

F (6 years): Responsibilities taken on. A good financial period. Domestic matters become important. Romantic interests possible.
FF: Overburdened with responsibilities.

G (7 years): Solitude needed at times. Tendency to secrecy. Finances good. Excellent period for study or research.
GG: Spending too much time alone.

H (8 years): Good period for business expansion. Financial trend is upwards. Can try too hard. Can establish independence.
HH: Over-ambitious at work.

I (9 years): Emotional period. Nervousness and delays possible. Many dramatic ups and downs. Creative opportunities always present.
II: Difficulty in getting things started.

J (1 year): A change of some sort. Financial prospects good. Indecision at times.
JJ: Over-activity leads to confusion.

K (2 years): Spiritually inspiring period. Partnerships are enhanced. Health may need attention. Unusual events.
KK: Emotionally sensitive.

L (3 years): Many new friends and social events. Good for creative purposes but may waste opportunities having fun.
LL: Over-indulging in pleasure.

M (4 years): Practical and realistic time. Needing to work hard. Finances improve slowly. Energy levels not high.
MM: Over-work. Rest needed.

N (5 years): Pleasurable period with exciting events. Travel indicated. Many changes possible. Adaptability enhanced. Finances fluctuate.
NN: Extreme restlessness.

O (6 years): Good period to study in. Domestic responsibilities accepted. Finances improve. A calm, sure, period.
OO: Emotionally drained by the problems of others.

P (7 years): Intellectual activities enhanced. Time spent alone is needed. Good business vibration if precautions taken.
PP: Behave at times too much like a hermit.

Q (8 years): Finances good. Unusual business ventures favoured. Eccentric time. Misunderstood by others.
QQ: Judged as over-eccentric.

R (9 years): Creative and compassionate period. Ambitions highlighted. Much confusion and emotion present. Delays at times.

RR: Endings and delays. A difficult time.

S (1 year): Circumstances change. Surprises. Often emotions are high. An active and ambitious period.
SS: Reversals likely.

T (2 years): Possible change of home. Partnerships prosper. Health needs watching. More sensitive and aware than usual.
TT: Over-tense.

U (3 years): Creative time. Enjoyable experiences associated with groups. Financial acumen is low. Confidence needs boosting.
UU: Confusion.

V (4 years): Important practical venture started. Personal power is marked in this period. Hard-working. Possibility of outstanding achievement.
VV: Plans too ambitious. Overworked.

W (5 years): Many changes happen. An adventurous period. Emotions need restraining. Travel likely. Interests change quickly.
WW: Scatters energy over many interests.

X (6 years): Home life enhanced. An unusual period. Public recognition possible. Romantic and love interests high.
XX: Accept sacrifices in some way.

Y (7 years): A need to choose a direction. Solitude needed to make life decisions. Spiritual awareness gained after confusion.
YY: Inability to take positive action.

Z (8 years): Fine financial prospects. Business ability enhanced. Unusual or psychic affairs attract. Unusual domestic conditions.
ZZ: Difficult domestic situations.

Note: Two or more Rs in transit during the same year can cause considerable delays; two or more Is have a similar effect, although not as severe. Love and compassion shown to others during these transits eases any difficulties.

THE EVENT NUMBER

The Event Number shows the essence, or the combined likely effect, of your current Transiting Letters. The numbers of these Transiting Letters are added together (fadically). For instance: A(1), R(9), and K(2) would give an Event Number of 3; H(8) and X(7) would give an Event Number of 6.

The Event Number and the Letters of Transit are analysed together.

Event Number 1: New beginnings. New starts. A fresh direction. An opportunity to start anew.

Event Number 2: Cooperation and partnerships. A quiet time. An opportunity to make friends.

Event Number 3: Life becomes joyful. A happy social period. An opportunity to be creative.

Event Number 4: Hard work and self-discipline. A practical period. An opportunity to achieve stability or put down roots.

Event Number 5: Surprising changes. Freedom is sought. Communication enhanced. An opportunity to try something new.

Event Number 6: Responsibilities taken on. Creativity is expressed. An opportunity to achieve a well-balanced life.

Event Number 7: Inner knowledge gained. Study and meditation enhanced. An opportunity to find your spiritual path. Unlooked-for victories.

Event Number 8: Goals can be reached. Rewards arrive if deserved. An opportunity to become more independent.

Event Number 9: Emotional period. Something ends. Idealistic time. An opportunity to gain understanding.

THE DAILY FORECAST

We have now calculated the main numbers used in predictive numerology, or the more accurate term: a numerological forecast. It is not a question of analysing one number but of combining accurately the effect of many.

Most of our days are a mishmash of emotions and events and our daily numbers usually reflect this. Occasionally the same number is repeated many times in a forecast; this indicates an important period; the qualities this number represents will determine the likely outcome of the day (or month, and so on).

A quick way to find the daily vibrations is to calculate the Universal Day, then find your Personal Day by adding your Goal Number to the Universal. The Universal Day shows the help you can get from others; the Personal Day shows what you can do to help yourself.

For instance: Universal Day 1, Personal Day 7 – good for initiating new projects with outside help but you may prefer to spend time alone thinking how to perfect your plans/life. If you should decide to act, the outcome could be successful in a materialistic sense (1 and 7 added together make 8).

For more detailed analysis you will need to write down all your predictive numbers. Include your Life Path for guidance. Here is one particular day for a man with a 5 Life Path:

Life Path 5	Universal Day 5
Cycle 7	Universal Month 9
Challenge 5	Universal Year 3
Turning Point 0	
Personal Year 6	
Personal Month 3	
Personal Day 8	
Transit Letter S(1)	
Transit Letter Z(8)	
Transit Letter G(7)	
Event Number 7	

At first glance it is a bewildering list of numbers. The important consideration is how these numbers affect the Life Path Number. The Life Path and Universal Day are both 5. This is an excellent day for this person to pursue his personal ambitions. The world is with him. His Personal Day being 8 shows he will need to set goals or strive ahead (5 and 8, while conflicting, are a dynamic combination). This is a purposeful day.

The following subtle vibrations affect his life over a longer period: the Universal numbers, all being odd, are harmonious with his Life Path; so also is his Personal Month. It is probably not an easy year for him as his Personal Year is 6 – responsibilities and domestic concerns will not please his 5 Life Path.

His Cycle and Event Number are the deep mysterious 7; he will think a lot about his personal motives during this period. The 7 vibration has a calming effect on the 5 but is harmonious. Unfortunately, this Cycle has a 5 Challenge behind it and he will find it harder to follow the dictates of his Life Path. He will conquer this as he ages. The period is good financially (G and Z) and some form of surprising change (the S) is likely during the year.

The overall look of this list is scattered, but this month should be lucky for him if he needs outside help (Life Path 5, Universal Year 3, Universal Month 9 – all numbers in harmony). The 7 Event Number coming in a 7 Cycle suggests the birthday year (from birthday to birthday) is important, if in a quiet way.

LUCKY NUMBERS

Many people have a favourite or lucky number. Often they do not know why they are attracted to it; sometimes it is a subconscious awareness of what that number represents. Believing in a 'lucky' number appears silly. The word 'significant' is a more accurate description of the effect the number has but the word 'lucky' conveys the positive possibilities that are achievable. It is a universally happy description.

The most significant vibration that affects you is your Life Path Number. It represents the day of your birth. It is the energy that first surrounded you when you emerged into the world. It is what you are most comfortable with. It shows you your easiest path, your direction, your opportunities, your talents. It is therefore your *lucky* number. No other number is so important to you. Whenever or wherever this number occurs in your life – the Universal Day, your Name Number, your Personal Year, or in anything – it represents opportunities that will be easier for you to take than they will be for someone with a different Life Path. Your Life Path Number is your main lucky number.

You have two other numbers of luck that are not as important: your Birthday Number is useful for personal or family matters; and the number of your Personal Year can be used effectively during its twelve months for luck in matters relating to what the number represents.

The following list indicates the kind of support *all* the numbers can give you when you are planning your life.

BEST NUMBERS FOR:

Artistic matters: 3 6 9

Attracting luck: 3 (or your Life Path Number)

Attracting money: 3 9

Attracting unsolicited help: 7

Business success: 1 4 8

Conserving Assets: 7

Creating Public Interest: 5

Developing friendships: 2 6

Developing independence: 1 5 7 8 9

Developing spirituality: 2 7 9

Domesticity: 2 6

Energy needed to work: 4

Following directions: 2

Fun and laughter: 3 5

Gardening: 4

Getting what you deserve: 8

Healthy balanced life: 6

Idealistic, dramatic or romantic matters: 9

Literary endeavours: 3 5 6 9

Love: 2 6

Making new friends: 3 5

Making own luck: 1

Managing money: 4 8

Marriage: 2 6

Musical endeavours: 2 3 6 9

New home: 4 6

Original enterprises: 1 5

Partnerships: 2 6

Planning or laying foundations: 4

Psychic matters: 2 7 9

Public recognition: 1 2 3 5 8 9

Religious ritual: 7 9

Research: 1 5 7

Seeking freedom: 1 5 7 9

Self-employment: 1 5 7 9

Selling goods: 5

Sexual expression: 3 5

Solitary matters: 7

Sporting events: 4 5 8 9

Taking on responsibilities: 6

To begin something: 1 5

To end something: 9

Travelling: 3 5 7 9

Working in teams: 2 4 6

13 · THE COMPLETE NUMEROLOGY PROFILE

Life consists not in holding good cards but in playing those
you do hold well.

Josh Billings

You have discovered all your important numbers. They may
appear to form a complex pattern. Everyone is not simply 'a
2' or 'a 6', just as they are not simply a Taurean or a Leo. You
may have one or two numbers that dominate your chart; this
makes it easier to analyse.

Put together all your numbers by making a list in this order:

1. Life Path
2. Birthchart
3. Lines on the Birthchart
4. Birthday
5. Goal
6. Vowel Number
7. Consonant Number
8. Name Number
9. Power
10. First Name Number

11. First Letter
12. First Vowel
13. Middle Letter
14. Last Letter
15. Intensity
16. Missing Numbers
17. Namechart
18. Submerged Characteristic
19. Temperament Chart

The charts of the Birthchart, Namechart and Temperament
Chart can be placed on a separate piece of paper but keep
the names on the list.

From your first number (your Life Path) work your way down the list (consulting the charts when you need to), analysing your strengths and weaknesses as you go. It is important you compare *all* your numbers and numerological patterns to how they relate to your Life Path Number. Do you have an easy or difficult chart? What areas need attention? Working with your numbers develops your self-awareness.

You may prefer to only list the main numbers (as set out in Chapter 10, p.86) and this can be less confusing. The main numbers are: Life Path; Birthday; Goal; Name Number; Vowel Number; Consonant Number; First Name Number; Power; First Letter, First Vowel; and Intensity.

After studying the above numbers, you can forecast any trends occurring in your life by listing your numbers of prediction. As we discovered (in Chapters 11 and 12) they are: your present Cycle; Challenge; Turning Point (if in operation); the Universal Year; Universal Month; Universal Day; Personal Year; Personal Month; Personal Day; Letters of Transit; and the current Event Number.

The Challenge, which represents a psychological attitude more than it does an opportunity or trend, is usually placed among the predictive numbers. This is because, for most people, it will usually change.

As an example we will look at the numbers of a Hollywood legend: Marilyn Monroe. She was born June 1st 1926 (6+1+1926 = 25, 2+5 = 7). Her birth date, her chosen name of Marilyn Monroe, and the record of her birth certificate are three undisputed facts among her many biographers. We will concentrate our analysis on these three.

NUMEROLOGY PROFILE: MARILYN MONROE

LIFE PATH 7

She was an individualist, needing time to herself each day. A perfectionist who probably disliked taking advice. The 7 learns by experience and makes its own mistakes. It dislikes working as part of a team. To those who knew her, her solitariness was a notable trait. It is quoted in many biographies. She once said: 'I would like to be more sociable than I am.' As a child she would often withdraw into herself and when working on film sets in later life was seen by many as a 'natural loner'.

This describes the holder of a 7 Life Path Number well but is far from her public image: the entertaining dumb blonde. But her image appears (accurately) in her Consonant Number (see below).

BIRTH CHART

	6 6	9
2		
1 1		

Chart 10. Marilyn Monroe's Birthchart

Numbers on the Birthchart

Two 1s: Expressive. Effective position for working in the public eye.

One 2: Perceptive and emotionally sensitive.

Missing 3: A fear of using creative expression.

Missing 4: Lacked practicality, careless over details.

Missing 5: Needing someone to motivate her.

Two 6s: Creative. Harmonious. Home-life was important: a

foster child who needed a secure home environment. This need would stay with her. It is at odds with her 7 Life Path which is not a domestic number. Conflicting domestic needs would occur in her life.

Missing 7: Dislike of being alone – this was negated by her 7 Life Path.

Missing 8: Carelessness and laziness over organization.

One 9: Of little significance; representing idealism common to everyone born at this time.

Lines on Birthchart

Missing 3–5–7: Encourages a nervous disposition. She would have been either extremely sceptical or welcoming of new ideas. Probably the latter.

Birthday 1

Leadership and a dislike of taking orders. Original people. With her 7 Life Path this created a strong individualistic streak. Her own concerns and needs would dominate her life.

Goal 7

She aimed to achieve self-knowledge, to be comfortable with herself when alone. Her three main birth numbers were 7,1,7, creating a powerful individuality. A person who would reject advice. 7 is not always an easy number – making things unnecessarily difficult for itself at times; sometimes it will sacrifice everything to have its own way. From her birth numbers this is not someone who would be easily manipulated. She would know what she wanted.

NAME CHART

Marilyn Monroe was enrolled at her school as Norma Jean Baker and it is *likely* this is the main spelling she used until she married her first husband at sixteen, Jim Dougherty. There is confusion over her various names. Recent biographers have chosen to spell Jean with an 'e' (Jeane) as she sometimes spelt it like this and it is the correct spelling on her birth certificate. What name she used consistently is a grey area. There are at least eight, possibly ten, used names at various times. For the famous nude calendar she modelled under the name Mona Monroe. As Marilyn Monroe she left her past behind so this is the name we will examine.

Vowel Number 7

This is a perfect complement to her 7 Life Path. She would have welcomed her Life Path opportunities. It reinforces the need for privacy that we see in the birth numbers. She kept her thoughts, her real needs, to herself. Seven has deep emotional needs but has difficulty in communicating them. This number helps the intuition develop and has a need to taste the experiences life has to offer. It experiences everything at first hand even if this creates uneasiness.

Consonant Number 3

Her public persona was different from the numbers we have examined so far. Here is the bright, scintillating 3 of the entertainer. Gregarious, the life of the party, someone who communicates fun, happiness and joy as a first impression. This would have been the first public image. Different from the 7, it is still – being an odd number – in harmony.

Name Number 1

The name, Marilyn Monroe, is harmonious with her 7 Life Path. The Name Number is also in harmony with her Vowel and Consonant Numbers. As Marilyn Monroe she would interact with people as a leader. She would make her way through life in an original way. Determination would underlie everything attempted.

The stress in her life (Life Path 7 subtracted from Name Number 1 = 6) would have shown up in her home or domestic life: a stress that is also shown between her Life Path and the two 6s on her Birthchart. Domestic harmony would have been difficult to keep hold of – as shown in her three marriages. This stress is compounded by her 1 Birthday, another number that is domestically uncomfortable.

Power 8

Her Life Path 7 and Name Number 1 added together create the number 8. A powerful trio. Ambition, originality, individualism and goal-setting all combined. Striving unflinchingly towards career success is the usual manifestation of this number. If for a moment we stop using fadic addition we then have a Life Path number of 25 and a Name Number of 73; add them together, again not using fadic addition, and we are left with a Power Number of 98. The following words total 98: 'Film Star' and 'Renowned' – this was the power that was easier to gain when she changed her name to Marilyn Monroe. Her 7 Life Path, striving to achieve perfection, enabled her to improve her acting by an intensive study of the 'method' school. The 7 here would not be satisfied by material success alone.

First Name Number 2

In her private life she would want a partner or companion. She probably felt some conflict here as her real needs for self-examination and solitude were suppressed. There is a big difference between the private and public aspects of this name.

First Letter M(4)

Encourages practicality, integrity and mood changes. Desires love and excitement.

First Vowel A(1)

Her first emotional reaction would have been assertive, taking action on her needs.

Middle Letter I(9)

Dramatic and romantic feelings could have become obsessive.

Last Letter N(5)

Affairs would have been concluded in an unpredictable way. A need for change.

Intensity 9 & 5

In Marilyn Monroe the strongest numbers are: 9, compassion, romance, idealism; and 5, communication, seeking change and freedom, plus sexuality.

Missing Numbers 2 & 8

The 2 is on her Birthchart, so it does not count. She had the 8 as her Power Number, which would have helped develop some organizational skills and financial acumen. The 3 and 7 missing on her Birthchart are contained in her name.

Namechart

Marilyn Monroe on this chart complements and balances her Birthchart. Try it and see. The 8 is still missing but she now has it as her Power Number.

Submerged Characteristic 4

This name helped bring practicality into play when needed.

TEMPERAMENT CHART

MENTAL 4: The name promoted logical thinking.
PHYSICAL 3: Life was faced in an artistic way.
EMOTIONAL 5: Emotional change was assisted.
INTUITIVE 1: Ideas would appear suddenly, creatively.

There are many letters on the Start line, giving good ability to create and no difficulty in continuing. Perhaps a need to try harder to finish projects at times.

SUMMARY

It is likely for her first sixteen years she used and was known as Norma Jean (without an e) Baker. This spelling of Norma Jean was used by two husbands, appeared on her first wedding invitation and was used by the woman who looked after her for her first eight years. We will assume it was the name she was known by (most of the time) until at sixteen she changed her name by marriage. Marilyn Monroe was created four years later. Here, we will briefly compare Norma Jean Baker to Marilyn Monroe.

When we look at her important numbers (as in the suggested list in Chapter 10) we see that as Norma Jean Baker the dominant number was the number 1 (occurring five times) with 5 and 7 appearing twice. As 7 was her Life Path, 1 and 7 would have been her two most important numbers. With so many 1s it would have been difficult for her not to over-emphasize the qualities of her 1 Birthday instead of those of her 7 Life Path.

As Marilyn Monroe, the important numbers achieve a better balance. Her most repeated numbers are 1 and 7 (both appearing three times) and she had a single number under every digit except the number 6; although 1 and 7 occur the same number of times, the 7s contain her Life Path. Seven becomes her strongest number. A fortunate occurrence.

For someone born June 1st 1926, Marilyn Monroe was a better name to live under than Norma Jean Baker. Her own free will would decide how she would ultimately act in life but this change in name made it easier for her to follow her true desires.

PREDICTIVE NUMBERS

For her Letters of Transit and Event Numbers we use the name as written on her birth certificate. This is Baby Norma

Jeane Mortenson. It was not necessary to write the word *baby* but it has been written down. Some numerologists would consider this divine guidance. Her mother's name Mortensen, has a different spelling (the vowels) than the version of it officially placed on Norma Jeane's birth certificate. But it is the official version, with mistakes and extraneous words, that is *always* used.

It is a confusing chart, but symbolically her first Event Number is a 3: the mark of the entertainer.

Only during three years in her entire life did she not have a Transiting Letter that did not represent the number 5. Five, the number of communication, freedom, and often associated with sexuality, was present for thirty-three of her thirty-six years. When we look at her First Challenge, we see it was also 5. Not only did life continuously bring her opportunities related to the five senses, but until the age of twenty-nine she would have needed to overcome the problems they represent. People with 5 dominant often attract occurrences that have a basis (if unconscious) in their sexuality.

Her First Cycle (to twenty-nine years) was a 6. There would have been the need for a secure home ever-present. She was brought up in various foster homes and an orphanage (which one could not forecast from numerology) but although the 6 Cycle would create a desire for 'domestic bliss', it conflicts with the 1s and 7s in her chart. Her Life Path 7 shows someone who is essentially a loner, whatever the other numbers say, and Marilyn Monroe's other numbers reinforce the individualism of the 7 and leadership of the 1.

Her predictive chart is not especially easy. Twenty-four of her years she had two or more of the same letters transiting. This can create too strong an effect and bring out the negative qualities of the numbers involved.

She married at an early age the son of a neighbour, Jim Dougherty. This was during a 5 Personal Year and one could speculate it was a way for her to seek freedom. She had a 7 Event Number, the Universal Year was 7, and she was sixteen years old – 16, a fadic 7. The 7 of her Life Path keeps appearing at significant occasions in her life. Four years later, during a 9 Personal Year (endings), she divorced him in Las Vegas.

The most important day in her life was July 16th 1946. She walked into the office of Ben Lyon, who was chief talent scout at Twentieth Century-Fox. He is reported to have looked at her and said: 'Honey, you're in pictures.'

The day was the 16th – a 7; the month was July – a 7; the Universal Day (7.16.1946) was a 7; her Personal Month was a 7. Her lucky number repeated four times combined with the ending of her old life as reflected in the number 9: her Personal Year was 9; her Event Number was 9; the Universal Month was 9. The numbers 7,7,7,7, and 9,9,9, combined with the freedom-seeking 5 of her Personal Day. Within fourteen days she had a seven-year film contract, a new name, new image and new life. She was about to become a 'film star' – a word seen in her new Power Number. She became Marilyn Monroe.

That ever-imitated photograph of her – standing over a sidewalk grating, white dress billowing around her waist – is from her arguably most famous film 'The Seven Year Itch'. The film title also totals a fadic 7. Film production stopped on a 7 Universal Day; and the première was just after her First Turning Point, another 7, came into force.

To select briefly some important events: in 1953 she received the 'Photoplay Gold Medal', at the time a prestigious award. She was in a 7 Personal Year with a 7 Event Number in transit.

She formed her own production company at the age of 27 in the same 7 Personal Year but with an 8 Event Number now in transit. Eight, the natural number of the executive and business world.

In 1956, after fighting the infamous studio system, she returned on her own terms, now a powerful figure in possession of an impressive contract. She was in a 1 Personal Year (new starts); the start also of a 1 Cycle; a 4 Event Number may seem limiting but here it had the powerful full number of 22 (considered a Master Number) behind it (masterful achievements); and her First Turning Point was now activated – a 7.

In June of the same year she married the playwright, Arthur Miller – himself a Life Path 7. In later life the late

President Kennedy is reported to have been a friend – another 7 Life Path.

She died during a 7 Personal Year at the age of 36 in mysterious (a word often associated with the number 7) circumstances. Her death was reported to the police in the early hours of August 5th 1962. Intriguingly, her grandmother, Della Hogan Monroe, was committed to a mental institution 35 years earlier (7 fives make 35) on August 4th 1927 – a 4 Universal Day. As Marilyn died the Universal Day was 4 and she had a 4 Event Number in force. Numerology cannot predict death and the calendar number of the day seems more fitting for the departure of a 'sex goddess', a 5.

MASTER NUMBERS

We have looked at the elements of conventional numerology where fadic addition is *always* used. But the numbers behind the final numbers *are* important and you will always find useful information if you examine them. For instance: 31 behind the number 4 will show a more creative 4 (the influence of the 3) than a 4 with 40 behind it.

Using the full numbers of the alphabet to find the numbers of words (LOVE would be: 12 + 15 + 22 + 5 = 54) reveals information that is hidden when fadic addition only is considered. This is an informative area that you might like to explore further.

Some numerologists do not use fadic addition when the number is a Master Number. The Master Numbers are: 11,22,33,44,55,66,77,88,99. Normally, those who use Master Numbers only consider 11 and 22 and reduce the rest to their fadic numbers. The Master Numbers are traditionally believed to contain more powerful vibrations than other numbers. Here are their meanings:

11 Inspired and spiritual or fanatical and dishonest.
22 The Master Achiever or the big-time crook.
33 Creative and responsible or the martyr.
44 Material achiever or destructive and over-worked.
55 Energy and intelligence or extreme restlessness.

66 Harmony and artistry or opinionated and meddlesome.
77 Mystery and originality or procrastination and dreaming.
88 Ambition and philanthropy or greed and ruthlessness.
99 Idealistic leader or destructive tyrant.

LUCKY COLOURS

Many books on numerology list *lucky* colours for various numbers. The colour you are given depends on which book you are reading at the time. It depends on the author and the tradition they are writing of.

The following selection is based on the generally accepted effect of the various colours. It is not infallible. If you wish to become more practical, or activate the quality of the number 4, and red represents practicality to you – ignore this list and wear red. What follows is a guideline. Good luck.

LIFE PATH COLOURS

1. Red for courage. Orange for activity. Gold for leadership. Yellow/Green for change.
2. Pink for love. Light blue for peace. Violet for inspiration. Grey for attention to detail.
3. Red for attraction. Maroon for pleasure. Yellow for joy. Violet for creativity.
4. Orange for activity. Brown for security. Dark blue for self-reliance. Grey for practicality.
5. Maroon for sensuality. Yellow for communication. Yellow/green for change. Light blue for freedom.
6. Pink for love. Blue for serenity. Green for balance. Violet for creativity.
7. White for individuality. Light blue for analytical thought. Dark blue for intellectualism. Indigo for intuition.
8. Red for ambition. Orange for activity. Dark blue for self-reliance. Black for authority.
9. Pink for love. Red for idealism. Violet for creativity. Purple for spirituality.

When we understand our motivation and our desires we are poised to achieve greater fulfilment in our lives. Numerology is a traditionally based system that can help achieve this. There are others. I hope you find the knowledge held within numbers gives you the key to open many doors.

The bibliography contains many fine works; for further reading you may find any of the following five books an interesting place to start from: the traditional classic, *Your Days are Numbered* by Florence Campbell; the excellent *Secrets of the Inner Self* by Dr David A. Phillips and *Numerology: Key to the Tarot* by Sandor Konraad; Julia Line's *Numerology Workbook* covers more ground than most; and Shirley Blackwell Lawrence's *Behind Numerology* provides insight into the field of word analysis.

Numerology is a numerical analysis of life. It is up to you how you use it. May your counting be correct and your numbers lucky.

BIBLIOGRAPHY

Anderson, Mary, *Numerology: The Secret Power of Numbers*, Aquarian Press, Wellingborough, 1979.

Andrews, Ted, *The Magical Name*, Llewellyn Publications, St Paul, MN, 1991.

Andrews, Ted, *The Sacred Power in Your Name*, Llewellyn Publications, St Paul, MN, 1990.

Bek, Lilla and Holden, Robert, *What Number Are You?*, Aquarian Press, London, 1992.

Bernstein, Henrietta, *Cabalah Primer*, DeVorss & Co, Marina Del Rey, 1984.

Bishop, Barbara J., *Numerology: The Universal Vibrations of Numbers*, Llewellyn Publications, St Paul, 1990.

Blackwell Lawrence, Shirley, *Behind Numerology*, Newcastle Publishing Co, North Hollywood, 1989.

Bosman, Leonard, *The Meaning and Philosophy of Numbers*, Rider & Co, London, 1932.

Buess, Lynn M., *Numerology for the New Age*, DeVorss & Co, Marina Del Rey, 1987.

Bunker, Dusty, *Numerology and Your Future*, Para Research, West Chester, 1987.

Campbell, Florence, *Your Days are Numbered*, DeVorss & Co, Marina Del Rey, 1987.

Cheiro, *Cheiro's Book of Numbers*, Prentice Hall Press, New York, 1988.

Coates, Austin, *Numerology*, Granada Publishing, London, 1978.

Cooper D. Jason, *Understanding Numerology*, The Aquarian Press, Wellingborough, 1990.

Culbert, S.J., *Your Lucky Number*, W. Foulsham & Co, London, 1986.

Culbert, Steven John, *The Right Name for Baby*, W. Foulsham & Co, 1988.

Davies, Rodney, *Fortune Telling with Numbers*, The Aquarian Press, Wellingborough, 1986.

Eisen, William, *The Cabalah of Astrology*, DeVorss & Co, Marina Del Rey, 1986.

Fitzgerald, Arlene J., *Numbers for Lovers*, Manor Books, New York, 1974.

Godwin, Joscelyn, *The Mystery of the Seven Vowels*, Phanes Press, Grand Rapids, 1991.

Goodman, Morris C., *Modern Numerology*, Fleet Press Corporation, New York, 1945.

Goodwin, Mathew Oliver, *Numerology: The Complete Guide*, Vols 1 & 2, Newcastle Publishing Co, North Hollywood, 1981.

Gruner, Mark, and Brown, Christopher K., *Numbers of Life*, Taplinger Publishing Co, New York, 1978.

Hitchcock, Helyn, *Helping Yourself with Numerology*, Wolfe Publishing Ltd., London, 1972.

Hoffstein, Robert M., *A Mystical Key to the English Language*, Destiny Books, Rochester, 1992.

Jain, Manik Chand, *Birthday Numerology*, Sagar Publications, New Delhi, 1973.

Javane, Faith, *Master Numbers: Cycles of Divine Order*, Whitford Press, West Chester, 1988.

Javane, Faith, and Bunker, Dusty, *Numerology and The Divine Triangle*, Whitford Press, West Chester, 1979.

Johari, Harish, *Numerology: With Tantra, Ayurveda and Astrology*, Destiny Books, Rochester, 1990.

Jordan, Juno, *Numerology, The Romance in Your Name*, DeVorss & Co, Marina Del Rey, 1978.

Kiley, Shirlee and Gordon, Rochelle, *Your Name is Your Destiny*, Pan Books, London, 1984.

Konraad, Sandor, *Numerology: Key to the Tarot*, Whitford Press, West Chester, 1983.

Kumar, Ravindra, *Secrets of Numerology*, Sterling Publishers, New Delhi, 1992.

Le Gette, Bernard Spencer, *Numera: The Craft of Numerology*, Pan Books, London, 1976.

Line, David and Julia, *The Book of Love Numbers*, The Aquarian Press, Wellingborough, 1986.

Line, Julia, *The Numerology Workbook*, The Aquarian Press, Wellingborough, 1985.

Phillips, Dr David A., *Secrets of the Inner Self*, Angus & Robertson, Australia & London, 1981.

Rael, Joseph E. and Sutton, Lindsay, *Tracks of Dancing Light*, Element Books Ltd, Shaftesbury, 1993.

Rice, Paul and Valeta, *Potential: The Name Analysis Book*, Samuel Weiser Inc., York Beach, 1987.

Sachs, Bob, *The Complete Guide to Nine Star Ki*, Element Books Ltd, Shaftesbury, 1992.

Sepharial, *Kabalistic Astrology*, Newcastle Publishing Co, North Hollywood, 1981.

Seton, Julia, *Western Symbology*, The Rally, London, 1933.

Simpson, Jean, *Hot Numbers*, Hodder and Stoughton, U.S.A., 1987.

Stebbing, Lionel, *The Secrets of Numbers*, New Knowledge Books, Sussex, 1963.

Stein, Robin, *Your Child's Numerology*, Futura Publications, London & Sydney, 1987.

Stein, Sandra Kovacs, *Instant Numerology*, Newcastle Publishing Co, North Hollywood, 1985.

Stein, Sandra Kovacs and Schuler, Carol Ann, *Love Numbers*, Sphere Books Ltd, London, 1982.

Strayhorn, Lloyd, *Numbers and You*, Ballantine Books, New York, 1987.

Tatler, John, *The Cycles of Time*, Prism Press, Bridport, 1990.

Taylor, Ariel Yvon, *Numerology Made Plain*, Newcastle Publishing Co, 1973.

Taylor, Ariel Yvon and Hyer, H. Warren, *Numerology: Its Facts and Secrets*, Sagar Publications, New Delhi, 1973.

Tono, Helen, *It All Adds Up To Love*, Bantam Books, London, 1989.

Tuli, Mahan vir, *Numbers and Your Fortune*, Sagar Publications, New Delhi, 1992.

Valla, Mary, *The Power of Numbers*, DeVorss & Co, California, 1985.

Vaughan, Richard, *Numbers as Symbols for Self-discovery*, CRCS Publications, Sebastopol, 1973.

Warne, H.C.S., *Everyman's Numerology*, 1951.

Young, Ellin Dodge and Schuler, Carol Ann, *The Vibes Book*, Samuel Weiser, New York, 1979.

INDEX